STRINE

Fraffly Well Spoken
Fraffly Suite
Fraffly Strine Everything
The Scrambled Egghead

STRINE

LET STALK STRINE
AND
NOSE TONE UNTURNED

AFFERBECK LAUDER
Professor of Strine Studies, University of Sinny

Illustrated by Al Terego

URE SMITH
SYDNEY · AUCKLAND · LONDON

Publisher's Note

Strine has sold over 15,000 copies and has been
reprinted six times.

Distributed by Gary Allen Pty Ltd,
15 Nowill Street, Condell Park, NSW 2200

Published by Ure Smith, Sydney
a division of RPLA Pty Ltd
176 South Creek Road, Dee Why West, NSW, Australia 2099

First published in this form 1982
Reprinted 1982, 1983, 1984, 1985, Ure Smith 1985, 1987
© Copyright Alistair Morrison 1982
Produced in Australia by the Publisher
Printed by Everbest Printing Co. Ltd, Hong Kong

National Library of Australia Cataloguing-in-Publication Data

Lauder, Afferbeck
 Strine.

 Combined two previously published works by the
 same author: Let stalk strine, Sydney: Ure Smith,
 1965; Nose tone unturned, Sydney, Ure Smith, 1966.
 ISBN 0 7254 0601 1

 I. English language in Australia. I. Title.
 II. Title: Let stalk strine. III. Title: Nose
 tone unturned.

427'.994

LET STALK STRINE

A lexicon on modern Strine usage

ABOUT THE AUTHOR

Afferbeck Lauder was born in Mairlben to humble parents of noble hood. He very early in life astounded his keeper by displaying his extraordinary gift for languages. When he was only two days old he could read Scrabble, and three days later he learned to speak Strine. His first words to his startled parents were, 'Hey, youse! Gimmier lickerish trap an some chicken—an look, fellers, no hens.'

At the early age of three months he composed, and dedicated to his mother, the song entitled 'Thanks for the Mammary', which is still sung by Strines on Mother's Day. At the age of five he was appointed professor to the newly created School of Strine Studies at Ezz Rock.

Handicapped throughout his life by having been born with a rare and curious malformation of what is believed to be his head, he was for many years unable to read or write without the aid of powerful trinoculars. His output, nevertheless, has been enormous. Publications include: 'Some Lesser-known Vowel Sounds among Cable Tram Gripmen', 'There Snow Datter Batcher—Yerron Yerrone', and 'Little Lauder's Lexicon'.

Asked about his hobbies, Professor Lauder replied, 'Well, I do have a hobby horse, but I'm really more interested in such simple pastimes as word-botching, wolf-whistling and just sin in the sun.'

ACKNOWLEDGEMENTS

The author expresses his grateful acknowledgements to the *Sydney Morning Herald*, in which much of the material in this book originally appeared. He would also like to thank the hundreds of *Herald* readers who so kindly wrote to him offering valuable criticism and advice, and who submitted so many unsolicited Strine words and phrases.

He would also like to express his warmest thanks to the following people, animals and things for their help in a variety of ways:

To the pioneers: C. J. Dennis and Colin Wills.

To his wife, who stood by him, no matter what they said; to his psychiatrist; to his goldfish; and to his dog who answered the telephone and did all the typing.

And to the inventors and/or manufacturers of the following, without whose existence this book could never have been written: Espresso coffee; Miltown; the lightweight telephone; anti-noise earplugs; money; *Roget's Thesaurus;* carbon paper; girls; and the little bits of cotton wool that they put in the tops of bottles of capsules.

INTRODUCTION

It was recently reported* that while the English writer Monica Dickens was authographing copies of her latest book as they were being bought by members of the public in a Sydney shop, a woman handed her a copy and said, 'Emma Chisit'. Thinking that this was the woman's name, Monica Dickens wrote: 'To Emma Chisit' above her signature on the flyleaf. The purchaser, however, in a rather more positive voice, said, 'No. Emma Chisit?' Eventually it became clear that she had been speaking Strine, and had used the Strine equivalent of the English phrase, 'How much is it?'

The misunderstanding was due to the fact that Miss Dickens had never been told that while Strines are often able to understand and read English they usually speak only Strine.

This incident made a profoundly disturbing impression on me. I realized that while we all speak Strine fluently and are able to understand each other without much difficulty, there did not seem to be any reliable and comprehensive dictionary of the language available for use by visitors, students, New Strines and people who speak only English.

It is obvious that incidents such as the above must cause endless misunderstanding, discord and international friction. This little book is an attempt partly to fill this gap.

*Sydney Morning Herald, 30th November, 1964.

LET STALK STRINE

Air Fridge: A mean sum, or quantity; also: ordinary, not extreme. As in: The air fridge person; the air fridge man in the street.

Airman: *see* Semmitch.

Airpsly Fair Billis: Quite pleasant (*see also* Naw Shaw).

Airp's Trek: Mon painting in the ark ellery. (*See also* Contempry.)

Aorta: The English language contains many Greek, Latin, French, Italian and other foreign words, e.g. valet, vampire, vaudeville, vox-humana, hippocrepiform, etc. Strine, similarly, is richly studded with words and phrases taken from other, older tongues. Many of these have, with the passage of time, come to possess meanings completely different from their original ones. Two typical examples are the German words Eiche (Pronounced i-ker; meaning oak-tree) and Ersatz (pronounced air-sarts; meaning substitute). Both these are now Strine words, and are used in the following manner: 'Eiche nardly bleevit', and 'Ersatz are trumps, dear, yegottny?'

However, it is English which has contributed most to the Strine vocabulary. Strine is full of words which were originally English. Aorta is a typical example.

Aorta (pronounced A-orta) is the vessel through which courses the life-blood of Strine public opinion. Aorta is a composite but non-existent Authority which is held responsible for practically everything unpleasant in the

Strine way of life; for the punishment of criminals; for the weather; for the Bomb and the Pill; for all public transport; and for all the manifold irritating trivia of everyday living. Aorta comprises the Federal and State legislatures; local government councils; all public services; and even, it is now thought, Parents and Citizens' Associations and the CSIRO.

Aorta is, in fact, the personification of the benevolently paternal welfare State to which all Strines—being fiercely independent and individualistic—appeal for help and comfort in moments of frustration and anguish. The following are typical examples of such appeals. They reveal the innate reasonableness and sense of justice which all Strines possess to such a marked degree:

'Aorta build another arber bridge. An aorta stop half of these cars from cummer ninner the city—so a feller can get twirkon time.'

'Aorta mica laura genst all these prairlers and sleshers an pervs. Aorta puttem in jile an shootem.'

'Aorta stop all these transistors from cummer ninner the country. Look what they're doone to the weather. All this rine! Doan tell me it's not all these transistors—an all these hydrigen bombs too. Aorta stoppem!'

'Aorta have more buses. An aorta mikem smaller so they don't take up half the road. An aorta put more seats innem so you doan tefter stann all the time. An aorta have more room innem—you carn tardly move innem air so crairded. Aorta do something about it.'

Ark Ellery: *see* Airp's Trek.

Arm Arm: A child's appeal to its mother for help. As in: 'Arm arm, makim stop.'

Ashfelt: Asphalt.

Assprad: Excessively preoccupied with domestic order and cleanliness. As in: 'She's very assprad—she keeps

Water bat
jars-chewer nigh
Goa
natter teat night?
Jarssa touvers.
Wicker deffer
few drinxer
Nairn F.T.

Well
I doan fee
larp twit treely.
I beenin
tair nawl die.
Hair bat
chew calmer nova
to mipe lice?
Wicked F. Teat
mipe lice

Rome looking lovely.' This is a feminine adjective only; there does not appear to be any exact masculine equivalent, although the noun Hairndiman conveys something of the same meaning. Strine women may be assprad; Strine men may be hairndimen; or 'clever with their hens'. (*See also* Gloria Soame.)

Baked Necks: A popular breakfast dish. Others include emma necks; scremblex; and fright shops.

Bandry: Marking a limit, or border. As in: 'Yadder job as a bandry rider.'

Bare Jet: A phrase from the esoteric sub-language spoken by Strine mothers and daughters. As in: Q: 'Jim makier bare jet, Cheryl?' A: 'Narm arm, nar chet.'

Bim-Bye: To have been attacked. As in: 'Arm, arm, I've bin bim-bye a bull joe'; or 'He was having a laidan when he was bim-bye a fahl-web spider.'

Blue, Hala: Famous Strine soprano. Hala Blue and Andy Kleimags first appeared together as a light opera team in 1907 in *Snow White and the 700 Decibels*. Since that time, until the outbreak of television and the subsequent merciful decline of musical comedy, this ever-popular team has captured the hearts of Strine audiences whenever they appeared.

Even 'Old Vienna' type productions could not dampen the enthusiasm of their many faithful fans. Hala Blue as La Stentoretta in *The Shriek and the Cholera Tourer* was, to put it mildly, unforgettable.

For seventeen years this talented couple successfully toured the country, playing always to packed houses, in the roles of Dr. Yes and Little Miss Noma in 'Mam Barfly and Ida'.

Boll; Boller: Glass container with narrow neck; e.g.

A boller brosser pearl; a sick sands boll; less cracker boll, etc.

Bran: A dark, brannish colour. Rairping piper is usually bran, as also are bombers in Sinny.

Chair Congeal: Bisexual adhesive used in making furniture. First mentioned in early Strine nursery-rhyme science fiction. Unfortunately it is not possible to reproduce here the unexpurgated version of the rollicking old ballad which has been handed down to us from the earthy, uninhibited people of earlier days. At the request of the Strine Literary Censorship Vigilance Committee blanks have been substituted for certain passages which might have offended the sensibilities of modern Strines.

Chair congeal went up the hill,
Blank, blank and blank with laughter,
Blank, blank and blank; but blank—the Pill.
Congeal came tumbling after.

Cheque Etcher: Did you obtain. As in: 'Where cheque etcher hat?' or 'Where cheque etcher dim pull, sonny? Where cheque etcher big blue wise?'

Cheque Render: An ornamental tree with blue flares.

Contempry: Mon painting, furniture, architecture, etc. As in: 'I'd have the aqua, Bev, it's more contempry.' Note: Airp's trek, contempry, mon, and sreelist are all more or less synonymous and interchangeable terms.

Corpse: *see* Harps.

Cummer Ninner: *see* Aorta.

Dare Debts: No-hopers; nark leds; rep bairgs; drongoes.

Deteriate: To grow worse, or inferior; to deteriorate.

Didgerie: A prefix, the exact meaning of which depends on the suffix which follows. This suffix is usually: do, dabat, or lee-meenit. As:

(a) Man, he plays the didgerie do real good.

(b) Didgerie dabat it in the piper?

(c) Didgerie lee-meenit or were you kidding?

Dimension: The usual response to 'Thenk you' or 'Thenk, smite.'

Dingo: A word with two separate, unrelated meanings. When intoned with equal emphasis on the syllables it is the negative response to the question 'Jeggoda?' As in:

Q: Jeggoda the tennis?

A: Nar, dingo. Sorten TV.

When, however, the emphasis is on the first syllable, dingo becomes a parliamentary term of mild reproof.

Dismal Guernsey: Dollars and cents.

Doan Lemmyaf: I do not want to have to. As in: 'Arn jew kids in bare jet? Emeny times die affter tellyer. Now doan lemmyaf to speak dear Ken.'

Ear's Eve: The festive occasion of 31st December. Each year, at midnight, Strines throughout the land perform the ceremony of joining hands with strangers and chanting 'Shoulder Quaint's Beef Cot' (also known as 'Fro-lang Zine').

Ebb Tide: Hunger; desire for food. As in: 'I jess dono watser matter, Norm, I jess got no ebb tide these dyes.'

Egg Jelly: In fact; really. As in: 'Well, there's nothing egg jelly the matter with her. It's jess psychological.'

Egg Nishner: A mechanical device for cooling and purifying the air of a room.

Emeny: *see* Doan Lemmyaf; Enemy; and Semmitch.

Enemy: The limit of. As in: Enemy tether. Not to be

confused with Emeny of the phrase 'Emeny jiwant?'

Eye-level Arch: The Strine method of ordering a meal in a restaurant. As in: 'Eye-level arch play devoisters Anna piner martyr sauce an tea', or 'Eye-level arch ching chair min an some Swissair pork.'

Fair Plessen: *see* Naw Shaw.

Fillum: Film.

Fipes: *see* Harps.

Fitwer Smeeide; Fiwers Youide; Whinecha: (Synonyms) If I were you I would. As in: 'Fitwer smeeide leave him. He saw-way sonn the grog, Annie carn work wily strinken.' or: 'Fiwers youide leave him, anide goan livner unit. He snore worthit trouble.' or: 'Whinecha leave him. He'll nebby any good. You know your selfies no good. You carng gon frever like this.'

Flares: Blooms, blossoms; e.g. corn flares, wile flares, etc., as in: Q: Wet cheque ettha flares? A: Gloria sarnthay. I gom airtat Sairf Nils.

Flesh in the Pen: Momentary brilliance. As in: 'Ar, stoo gooder last, Sairndra, it's jessa flesh in the pen.' The derivation of this curious phrase is obscure. General etymological opinion is that it has come down from the time when the early Strine settlers fashioned pens from goose quills — often without first removing the goose. The phrase is believed originally to have been, 'goosefiesh in the pen', meaning shaky or illegible writing (caused by the struggles of the goose).

Foo Fairies: Characters in a popular television commercial, 'Woo worse, Foo Fairies, the happy way to shop.'

Furry Tiles: Sick humour for kiddies. These are stories which begin with the words, 'One spawner time . . . '

and then describe in graphic and revolting detail various acts of murder, mayhem and treachery, such as ' . . . he drew out a sharp knife and cut off the head of the wicked brother', and 'At nightfall they came to the edge of a deep forest and the young maiden then did what the witch had told her—she cut out the young huntsman's heart and threw it down the well. Then she wept bitter tears and could not be comforted and they lived happily ever after.'

Because of their violence and gloomy horror such stories are, naturally, very popular with young children, and it is surprising that so few Strine furry tiles exist. Those that do are usually variations on the theme of 'If we are returned to power . . . ' or 'You may rest assured that I shall leave no stone unturned.'

Gadgeter: I would be most grateful if you would. As in: 'I'll gadgeter sew a bun ommy shirt', or 'Yeggo ninter tan? I'll gadgeter gepme some lickerish traps an some rise-up lides.'

Garbler Mince: Within the next half hour. Also Greetings. As in: 'I'll be with you in a garbler mince', or 'With the garbler mince of the Gem of Directors.' (*See also* Gobbler Mincer.)

Garment: An invitation to visit. As in: 'Garment seamy anile seward icon do.' And: 'Garment the garden, Maud, I mirrored the gaiter loan.'—*Tennyson.*

Gest Vonner: Well-known linguist, heard regularly on the Ibey Sea. (*See also* Naw Shaw; and Slidy.)

Gissa: 'Please give me . . . ' As in: 'Gissa lookcha alchbra.' This word is the subject of a curious sexual taboo; it may be used only by males. The female equivalent is Gimme, or Gimmier. As in: 'Gimmier nairm semmitchenna cuppa tea.'

Carmen F. T. Withers.
We revving
ching liffis.
Jellike ching liffis?
We F.N.B. Neffen
roe smeal slightly
wither tellion
the kitser nawl.
Yeckered
calm strife rom
work

Theng Saula Syme
butter monner
diet.
I fed a bitifer
gairstrick
stummick lightly.
Spin plier
nuppagenner bit.
Arlga mauve rafter.
Oliver
bye tweet first

Gloria Soame: A spurban house of more than fourteen squares, containing fridge, telly, wart wall carps, payshow, and a kiddies' rumps room. Antonym: Terror Souse (*q.v.*).

Gobbler Mincer: Greetings. As in: The gobbler mincer the season, or: With the gobbler mincer the author. (*See also* Garbler Mince.)

Gona Gota: To go. As in: 'They're gona gota Gundagai to get a gelding and they're gona gota gether.' or: Q: You gona gota Moun Barflo freester? A: Narm gona gota Mairlben, I'm stain with some frenset Blair Crock.

Gonnie: Do you have any? As in: 'Gonnie epples?', 'Gonnie forby three oregon?' 'Gonnie newsa Bev?'

Grade A: So-called 'fine' weather, i.e. an intolerably hot and blinding summer day; also, an important occasion. As in: 'It's a grade A for the Irish'; 'It's a grade A for the people of Fiver No'; 'It's a grade A for the Dairptic Mishner of Texation'.

Gunga Din: Locked out. As in:
A: I gunga din, the door slokt.
B: Hancher gotcher key?
A: Air, buttit spoultered on the inside. I tellyer I gunga din. Car more, nope-nit.

Harps: Thirty minutes past the hour. As: Harps two; harps four; harps tait; etc. Related words are: Fipes; temps; corpse. As: Fipes one; temps two; corpse four.

Header, Mary: Daughter of one of the early Strine graziers. She was responsible, after years of bitter struggle with the authorities, for the introduction of compulsory education for sheep. She thus lit a lamp which has continued to burn steadily down the years and many of today's famous Strine sheep must be grateful to her memory. One of her little lambs, Charles, who had followed her to school each day, eventually became an essayist and poet of considerable skill and composed the following song in memory of his sponsor:

Mary Header little lamb;
An intellectual nit.
It never passed its first exam
Because it couldn't sit.

So Mary Header little lamb
With vedgies and mint sauce.
'Oh, dearest lamb,' she cried, 'I am
As hungry as a horse.'

Hembairg: A bag, carried by all Strine women, for the transport of personal possessions such as money, cigarettes, lipstick and a hairnkie. (*See also* Wezzme.)

Hip Ride: Popular radio music. Note: Any tune played more than twice becomes known as 'heather hip ride' or 'numbwun hip ride'.

Hop Eyes: Pastry cases, containing gravy, and occasionally heated. The singular is hop eye, or hoppine sauce.

I Marfter: I am about to leave. As in: 'Well, I marfter tan now. I'll gadgeter turn the oven on at harps four', and 'I marfter see the Wizard.' (*See also* Gona Gota.)

Inner Narkup Luddaze: A builder's term, meaning: within the next seven or eight weeks. An elaboration of this phrase, 'Air smite, inner narkup luddaze for sure', means, in the building trade, within the next seven or eight weeks.

Jans: An opportunity. As in: 'He neffradder jans', or 'He neffrad Barclay's jans.'

Jareedna; Wairtsed: These terms, relating to the dissemination of news, cannot be translated individually as they always occur in close juxtaposition in conversations such as the following:
Q: Jareedna piper wairtsed abat the bushfires? (or: abat the universty stewnce?)
A: Nar, sorten TV (or: sorten Woomz Dye).

Jeep Yo: A large building in each capital city. Administered by the Peem Jeeze Department of the Commwealth Garment.

Jess Tefter; Lefter: It is necessary to. As in: 'She'll jess tefter get chews twit', or 'You lefter filner form.'

Jezz: Articles of furniture. As in: 'Set the tible, love, and get a coupler jezz.'

Kelly, Ned ('Our Ned'): A notorious artists' model. Also thought to have been a bushranger.

Laidan: A short rest after the midday meal; a siesta.

Larks, Girldie: Research into early Strine history and the origins of the Strine language has continued to yield a rich harvest. Creeping about and sneezing among the foetid pages of old manuscripts; listening at the keyholes of the better-informed; surreptitiously removing pages from Public Library books—all these activities, though necessary, are exhausting and dangerous. But to the dedicated searcher after truth the rewards more than make up for the hardships. Such a reward has been the recent chance discovery of the true facts about Girldie Larks and the Forebears, now told here for the first time.

Girldie Larks was an early Strine juvile dinquent tea nature, whose scandalous career has until now been

An ashy wonster
doop the sperrume
an the lairnge.
Enchy storkner bat
a rumps room.
It carng gon
marsh lonker.
Washy thing
kiam?

Weller
corset snop
my bizner sreely
but jeer
fiwers youide
poomy foot dairn
nide
teller weshie
get sawf

hushed up and whose evil character whitewashed by her sentimental, over-indulgent parents. Girldie Larks is now known to have been a psychopathic thief and tormentor of dumb animals. An associate of Little Red Robin and other hoods, she made the lives of our forebears intolerable by her continual raids into their territory—trespassing, stealing food and destroying property.

Her special victims appear to have been the upright and popular Behr family—Father, Mother, Baby and the silent and rather less well known Cammom Behr. Her savage depredations continued for some years until eventually, his patience exhausted, Cammom cried, 'A little Behr will fix her!' and he then cut out her heart and threw it down a well—this being the appropriate course of action in those days when there were so many wells about. (*See also* Furry Tiles.)

A typical example of Girldie Larks' vicious cruelty is immortalized in the following old Strine folk song:

Girldie Larks, Girldie Larks, where have you been?
I beat up London and vented my spleen,
And then I cummome menai harassed the Behrs;
I yay tarp their porridge and bro karp their chairs.
I savaged the beds and I tordan the fences
And frightened a little mouse out of its senses.

Laze and Gem: Usual beginning of a public speech. Often combined with Miss Gem. As in: 'Miss gem, laze and gem. It gives me grape leisure . . . '

Lenth: Length.

Letty Mare Fit: Let him have it. As in: 'Letty mare fit tiffy wonsit. Zarf trawly zonier kid.'

Lickerish: Licorice.

Londger Ray: Women's underclothing.

Major, the Big Horse-cart: The Strine patron saint of young married couples, or as they are sometimes indulgently known, 'nearlyweds'. How the big horse-cart major came to acquire his curious nickname is unknown; indeed much of his life and background is obscured by conflicting reports and cryptic half-truths. One thing, however, is certain and that is that he has always been associated with marriage and weddings. Today no self-respecting soloist at a Strine wedding can be restrained from singing that so well loved melody addressed to 'Big Horse-cart Major Mine'.

Mare Chick: Effects produced by the assistance of supernatural powers. As: Bleck mare chick; mare chick momence; 'Laugh, your mare chick spell is airfree ware.'

Marmon Dead: Parents. As in: 'I saw Marmon dead, Sandra, they'd love tier frommier.'

Miss Gem: Correct method of addressing a person chairing a meeting.

Money: The day following Sunny. (Sunny, Money, Chewsdy, Wensdy, Thursdy, Fridy, Sairdy.)

Nardly; Carn Tardly: *see* Aorta.

Naw Shaw: A district of suburban Sinny, extending from Klahra to Waitara.

Naw Shaw is also a dialect of Strine, very closely related to the dialects spoken at Trairk, Sath Yeah, Poym Piper, and Rare Dill in Kairmbra. Gest Vonner, the overseas visiting linguist, speaks fluent Naw Shaw. 'Airpsly Fair Billis' is a typical Naw Shaw phrase, meaning: Quite pleasant, or mildly enjoyable. Another interesting Naw Shaw term is 'Fair Plessen' which means much the same thing, as in: 'Oat wess mosen choiple—wee etta fair plessen Dane deed.'

Neffereffer: Never. As in: 'He neffereffer rurdafit.' Sometimes: Neffereffereven. As in: 'The referee neffereffereven nurda wordavit.'

Nerve Sprike Tan: Mental collapse due to conflict, anxiety, etc. As in: 'He never let sarp, marm. He'll ever nerve sprike tan the waze goane.'

Nipey: *see* Split nair dyke.

Numb Butter; Jessa (Synonyms): Only. As in: 'They're numb butter buncher drongoes', or 'He's jessa no-hoper.'

Orpheus Rocker: Psychopathic; neurotic; psychotic; slow; quick; eccentric; absent-minded; unstable; excitable; imaginative; introspective; creative; or in any way different.

Panam: Unit of weight. As: A panam inn smeat.

Porchy, George E.: The main character in one of those baffling and inconsequent nursery rhymes with which Strine parents have for so long brainwashed their unfortunate children. Nauseatingly coy and yet loaded with disturbing ambiguity, it has been conceived with the obvious intention of engendering a sense of bewildered insecurity in the psyche of the innocent child. For those who are unfamiliar with the rhyme, the authorized version is as follows:

George E. Porchy kissed the girls and made them cry
And doesn't know where to find them.
And his bullets were made of lead, lead, lead,
And cockle shells all in a row.

Note the unhealthy emphasis on sex—presented as something terrifying; something which makes one cry.

Euro merli.

Wez Jeck?

I thorty scona

geminner neffer

drink.

Whyndie geminnen

silo

eneffer drink?

N Hair jigger

tonn?

Noppaired.

Jeck seddy

woonker min.

Seddiwer slight.

He's

jar sporter

Noel toonar

fleeter

with twink arbies

anorlat

chairs

Note the equivocal melancholy of, 'doesn't know where to find them'. Note the neo-colonial imperialistic line about bullets; and finally those cockle shells—all in a row like a lot of undemocratic automata.

Surely this is calculated to corrupt and deprave. Surely children should be told only the clean, straightforward, realistic tales of violence and horror that their little minds crave, and which fit them so well for the world of today. All this provocative and menacing symbolism of bullets and cockle shells must surely induce nightmares and must inhibit the normal kicking of playmates' shins and the happy gouging out of little eyes.

Fortunately, recent research into early Strine history has brought to light important new facts about George E. Porchy. He was, in fact, just a lovable old poisoner and a great favourite of little girls everywhere. This means that the whole squalid incident of the cockle shells can be forgotten, and the rhyme rewritten somewhat as follows:

George E. Porchy kissed the girls
And wrapped them round with furs and pearls.
He stroked their cheeks and called them 'Honey'
And gave them little bags of money.
He gave them cognac with their coffee,
And, finally, some home-made 'toffee'.
He said, as rigor mortis followed,
'It must be something that they swallowed.'

Giorgio Eduardo Porchy was the only son of Allegro and Lucrezia Borgia, who migrated from Italy to this country in 1852 where they changed their name to Porchy and established a small poisoning and garroting shop in a prosperous goldmining town near Bendigo.

Giorgio, a bright boy with a happy nature, took to poisoning effortlessly. When he was twelve both his parents died suddenly in rather mysterious circumstances, and he immediately took over the shop, which he rapidly built up into a thriving business.

For a while he had a little trouble with the authorities, who tended to be rather conservative in their ways. Fortunately, however, the police sergeant and the local magistrate were both women—the handsome Durberville sisters, daughters of the local dairyman. This no doubt is the origin of the preposterous libel about 'kissed the girls and made them cry over spilt milk'. Anyway, the likeable young George soon won their hearts and married them. He soon inherited the dairy from their father, who had passed away unexpectedly an hour or so after the wedding breakfast, and he successfully combined the two businesses.

Eventually he became mayor, then local member, and finally a senator, and was for many years one of the most popular figures in the district.

After his murder the local citizens, whose number had by this time dwindled to about twenty-five, erected a monument to his memory in the form of a bronze statue holding aloft a smoking test-tube, and surrounded by a group of happy little girls waving arsenical lipsticks. Issuing from his smiling lips is an elegant bronze 'balloon' on which is inscribed his family motto: 'Spero non Taedium'—I hope I haven't Borgia.

Puck, Charlie Charm: A whimsical character in Strine folklore, about whom many amusing anecdotes are told. Charlie Puck is famous for having introduced the popular sport of sheep-stealing. Mentioned in the national anthem ('Where sat Charlie Charm Puck you've got in your tucker bag?').

Rare Dill: A district in Kairmbra.

Rare Wick: A suburb of Sinny; also a racecourse.

Rep Bairg: An irresponsible person. *See also* Dare Debts.

Retrine: Making an effort. As in: How to speak Strine without retrine.

Ridinghood, Red: An attractive auburn-haired young woman who lived in a bark hut on the goldfields during the 1850s. At the time of the following incident she was unmarried but had a middle-aged friend who used to visit her regularly because his plain, elderly wife didn't understand him. This friend was a bit of an old wolf. He wore well-polished handmade shoes and had long teeth and pointed ears, but he was kind to Red and used to give her presents, and always paid the rent of the hut, to which he had his own key. Red used to call him 'Wolfie' and 'Daddy', and tried not to yawn when he talked about himself and about what he had said to the Minister.

One day Red came home from a visit to her furrier and found her friend sitting up in bed with a shawl covering his head and face, leaving only his teeth and chins visible. Surprised, because she couldn't remember having seen the shawl before, Red said, 'What's the matter, Big Daddy? You got near acre somethink?'

'I think I musta picked up a virus, dear,' came the muffled, slightly falsetto reply. 'Also, me teeth are falling out, one after another—Oops, there goes another one!'—and a large, gamboge canine tooth fell onto the bed, where it lodged upright, quivering like a dagger.

Alarmed, but not yet suspicious, Red cried out, 'Gee, Wolfie, yorter tiger nipey sea or somethink.' But the figure on the bed beckoned to her, 'No, thanks, dear, jusker meeren help me back with this tooth.'

Red, suspicious, drew back in alarm. She was almost sure now that this creature was an intruder and, worse still, probably female. There was a tense silence for a few moments. Then Red moved quickly. Knowing that her life probably depended on speed; knowing that, momentarily, she held the advantage; certain at last that this was an impostor and knowing that there could be no substitute for wolf, she sprang at the menacing old doll on the bed and gave her a brisk clip over the left ear with an empty sherry bottle.

It was all over in seconds. The last of the teeth fell away, taking the shawl with them, and revealing the pitiful, cowering figure of her friend's plain, elderly wife.

'Don't hit me again, dear,' she whined, 'I didn't mean any harm. I was on me way to the dentist—I've had a lot of trouble with me teeth at that lately. You know how it is out here—nothing but damper and salt beef and that—no vedgies or anything. Anyway, zize saying, I was on me way to the dentist when I had one of me turns like, and I thought I'd come in and have a bit of a laidan till it passed. I didn't think you'd mind. I must have dropped off. Ooh, you must think I'm awful.'

She paused, smiled wanly at Red, and picked a piece of glass out of her ear. 'We haven't seen you for such a long time, dear,' she went on. 'Whine cher comoveren have tea with us one day soon. I was zony sane to Norm lar snite, you know, Norm, we oughter ask Red to comoveren have tea with us. The poor kid must be lonely all by herself in that hut and all.'

Red breathed more easily as her fears ebbed away. The old girl hadn't found out, then, about her friendship with Norm. She picked her way through the broken glass and teeth and helped her victim to her feet. 'Gee, Elsie, I'd no idea it was you. I'm real sorry. Lep me getcher a cuppa tea.' She fussed over her, covered her ear with band-aids and took her round to the dentist.

Norm never· came to see Red again, and after a few weeks she got a letter from the agent about the rent. But then Norm had always been frightened that people would find out—that there might be a scandal and he wouldn't be re-elected. Norm had always been so kind, though. Red was lonely for a while, but not for long—there were plenty of other wolves about on the gold-fields in those days.

Rigid VI: Early Strine king; sometimes called Quick Brown Fox or Tête d'Oeuf (or Rigid Egg-head). Rigid the Sixth was a devoted husband and father, and was also very fond of animals, in marked contrast to his predecessors who had spent most of their spare time shooting arrows into the wild bores who roamed the palace corridors.

Rigid was also something of an eccentric; he invariably spoke English to his subjects but tolerantly allowed them to reply in their native Strine tongue. This democratic monarch's sense of justice was so fastidious that he treated even the royal alphabet with scrupulous fairness, and whenever he spoke always allowed each letter to make at least one brief appearance. The following scene from Act II of *Rigid VI* reveals the confusion which occasionally resulted from this curious habit.

(SCENE: *The palace moat, dry now because of the continual drought. Enter, Rigid and John, carrying bags of superphosphate. From Rigid's golden crown hangs a row of little corks on strings. His companion brushes away the flies with a small branch of mulga. Both look hot and uncomfortable in their purple velvet robes.*)

Fune Mervered
like tucker
mofer
wah neefnink
we'd laugh to see you.
Jekyll
show yiz slides.
An we gossamer
Wendy skitty stoo

G-weed
laughter seam.
Butter dunnif
wickairn.
Altar pants
on Merv.
E. Sconofer seesoon
N.U. Nairtiz
snore
flotta do

R. The quick brown fox jumps over the lazy dog.

J. What dog, your mare-chesty? Snow dog ear mite.

R. Rigid the Sixth briefly views Jack's pink zombi quins.

J. Wasser matter with you, King? That was muncer go—and stop jumping, will yer. Snow dog ear I tellya—Give yer the creeps.

R. Quiet gadfly jokes with six vampire cubs in zoo.

J. Gaudy scone office rocker. Listen, King, zoos hev neffereffer even been inventor jet.

R. King Rigid and Queen Zoe believe the wolf may expect jams.

J. That sawright, King, we should have plennier jammer tome. Mine jew, the quins get through a coupla jars every dye though. Would golden syrup do? What wolf?

R. Jumpy zebra vows to quit thinking coldly of sex.

J. Jeez, so now we got zebras too. No wonder they're gonna hafter invent zoos. Look out, King, jump! It's that dog again.

R. Two fixed androgynes doze quickly on film job. I have spoken.

(*Exeunt, humming Waltzing Matilda and cracking gold-handled stockwhips.*)

Rise Up Lides: Sharpened steel wafers, now usually stineless, used for shiving.

Rye-Wye: A dialect spoken by the Trine tribe. Strine, like any other living language, is constantly changing as new words and phrases are evolved or introduced and as old ones fall into disuse. All languages, and Strine is no exception, also carry with them many local dialects and sub-languages.

These are usually more conservative than the mother tongue. Like the side eddies in a river they remain static and self-contained—almost unaffected by the main stream of the language, and thus they become increasingly cryptic and obscure.

Such a dialect is Rye-Wye, which is spoken only by the Trine tribes over the public address systems of metropolitan railway stations.

All attempts to decipher this esoteric dialect have so far been unsuccessful, and it is now believed that it is not understood even by the Trine tribes who speak it. Rye-Wye is, in short, a ritualistic chant, the purpose of which is not to inform but to frighten away any passengers or other hostile spirits who may be lurking in the underground. For this reason it is not only terrifyingly loud but also breathtakingly dissonant. The following are typical examples:

(a) 'Awe lathers trine nair stannenat num-rye teen plafform pliz. Istrine term night sear. Awe lattpliz.'
(b) 'Nuffor plafform nawshawtrine stomming milce point naw sinny chasswood norl staish toresby.'
(c) 'Trine num-rye teen plafform gerster rare fern, bird and strair feel lonely.'

Sag Rapes: Anything which one wants but is unable to reach.

Sander's Lape: In a state of suspended animation. As in: 'Doan mica noise, Norm, the kiddies are Sander's lape.'

Saw Bat: Past tense of the verb to read. As in: 'I saw bat it in *Pix*', or 'I saw bat it in Sairdy's piper.'

Scared Saul: Mythical hero. Believed to have been the originator and spiritual head of the Boy Scat movement. This movement, so popular with Strines and New Strines alike, embraces also the Gurgides, Sea Scats, Brannies and Carbs. Scared Saul (known to his intimates as Jobber Bob) is thought to have been in some way related to Gloria Sarah Titch (*q.v.*). The meeting place and local centre of Scat activity is known everywhere today as the Scared Saul.

Scettin Lairder: It is becoming louder. (*See also* Scummin Glerser.)

Scona: A meteorological term. As in: Scona rine; scona clear up; scona be a grade A; etc.

Scummin Glerser: Approaching. As in:
Q: Jeer that noise, Norm? Wodger reckna tiz? Whateverit tiz, scettin lairder—scummin glerser.
A: Tsawright, dear, tsonia wisspring jet.

Semmitch: Two slices of bread with a filling in between, e.g. M-semmitch; semmon semmitch; chee semmitch. When ordering semmitches the following responses are indicated:
A: Sell semmitches?
B: Air, emeny jiwant?
A: Gimmie utter martyr and an airman pickle. Emma chisit? (or Emma charthay?)
B: Toon nimepen slidy. (or Threem form smite. A man is always expected to pay more for food than a woman is.)

Sex: Large cloth bags used as containers for such things as potatoes, cement, etc. As: Sex of manure, corn sex, etc. Also known as heshing bairgs.

Shablay: Chablis.

Share: Bathroom water spray. As in: 'Wine chevver cole share?' or, 'I think I'll ever shy venner not share.' Also: Rain. As in: Scadded shares and thunnerstorms.

Sick Snite: *see* Soup-marked Money.

Slidy; Smite: The feminine and masculine suffixes of the terms, 'Theng slidy' and 'Theng smite' (meaning:

Sarn's
calmer nairt.
Scona beer
gloria sty.
Mine jute still
scold zephyr.
Cheat was scold
la snite

Weller corset
Saul-wye school
linnermore
ninx.
Buttered swarm
nuddite-time.
Spewffle
climb a treely

Thank you, madam, and Thank you, sir). It is interesting to compare these terms with a similar one used by Gest Vonner and other overseas visitors — Thairnk yoch. As in: 'Thairnk yoch for the orp tune tare . . . ' (*See also* Naw Shaw.)

Sly Drool: An instrument used by engineers for discovering Kew brutes and for making other calculations.

Smarfit, Lilma: Early Strine health faddist and fetch-terrian. While still in her teens Miss Lilma Smarfit inherited the huge Smarfit chain of health-food stores—retail distributors of curds, whey, apple vinegar and molasses. Uncompromising in her love of vegetables and by nature obsessively ruminative, she devoted her long life to the cause of fetch-terrianism. Many nursery rhymes have been written about her exploits. The following is perhaps the best known:

Lilma Smarfit sat on a tarfit,
Digesting a bushel of hay.
She cried, 'I'm a bird
Who's addicted to curd,
And I'm to be Queen of the Whey.'

In spite of her fierce devotion to cellulose and dairy produce, Lilma Smarfit is known to have been an associate and consort of such gourmets and voluptuaries as little Jack 'Thumbs' Horner and George E. Porchy.

Snow White and the Severed Wharves: Snow White was a beautiful young Strine secret service agent. In private life she was a doctor of philosophy and a connoisseur of immersion heating. As a counter-spy (officially known as 004), she was noted for her dexterity with the hypodermic syringe and for her unswerving promiscuity in the service of her country.

Her most remarkable attributes, however, were her extraordinarily powerful lungs, which she used to great advantage whenever mouth-to-mouth anti-resuscitation was the only way to escape from the embraces of a no longer useful admirer. This high-pressure method was rather frowned on by her more conservative colleagues but it was undeniably effective; her victim just dilated like a sunfish and became entangled in the chandeliers, or drifted over the horizon in whatever direction the wind happened to be blowing.

It was a dull, grey autumn afternoon when Snow White left the Colonel's office. She stepped into her roller skates, and picked her way carefully through the traffic to the middle of the road. Skating along the centre line of a main highway usually calmed her turbulent spirit and gave her a sense of purpose and fulfilment. But today, somehow, she felt troubled and uneasy.

The Colonel's warning was still ringing in her ears. 'No more lust, Buster, I trust you. It's a must,' he had said, putting down the rhyming dictionary and lighting her cigar. 'Carry two Mausers in your trousers, and pack a new Luger with the nougat.'

Snow White knew what lay behind that friendly half-smile which contrasted so oddly with his grey, intelligent eyes, obscured now by the large empty prune can with which he always concealed his face from his subordinates. Poor James, she thought, how sensitive he still is about having no nose. His voice droned on, ' . . . and your teeth will be sharpened before you leave. That is all.' He paused and spoke a few words into the intercom.

He had briefed her well, she thought to herself as she overtook a large black sedan filled with Asians carrying cameras. Her mission was simple, but dangerous. She was to make her way undetected into 'their' territory, destroy the fleet of mini-submarines, and cut loose the floating wharves at Vitamin Bay. That was all. Simple enough, heaven knows—yet her uneasiness persisted.

Suddenly she threw away her cigar, put out her right arm and pulled sharply into the kerb at the left. She made her way thoughtfully towards a small, unobtrusive building which bore a large sign: 'Day Old Pullets—Hot Water—Ears bashed Wile-U-Wate—Cocker Puppies—Clean Toilets—Devonshire Teas'. She rapped on the boarded-up window with a roller skate. 'Are you there, James?' she called softly. There was no answer. She went round to the locked door, put her lips to the keyhole and blew out the lock. She stepped quietly inside. The Colonel was already there. She took him in her strong arms and kissed him fiercely on the prune can immediately above the words, 'Contains no preservatives'. He snuggled close to her and gurgled tinnily. She took his hand and together they walked along the narrow catwalk towards the submarines.

Snow White patted the Luger inside her armpit, and sniffed cautiously at the outgoing tide. There wouldn't be much time, she thought. She bent down and bit through the first cable with her powerful teeth and watched the grey hull sink slowly out of sight into the mud.

She looked around her. It was almost dark now, and the Colonel appeared to be asleep. She smiled grimly as she scrabbled among the barnacles, searching for the second cable. Suddenly, without warning, a blinding light flashed into her eyes, and a suave, unctuous voice broke the silence: 'Weaner rup this sprogram to bring you an important annancement from the Sinny Cricket Grand. New Sath Wiles are orlat for

Mr Terego!
Dint note was
ute first.
Dint
U.U. Steffer
beard?
I thaw
chetterlong
beard

Essa Dibbet
me wife
sediwer
skettin twold
twearer beard.
Shiss edit mimey
look lichen
Noel
office boy

three unren twen yite.' The menacing voice chilled her, and her hand gripped the Luger. 'The forecast for tomorrow is for scadded shares and Sathie's twins. An now we return you to this chewdio.' There was a click, then silence. Once more she was in darkness.

She was alone now; the Colonel had disappeared. At last she found the second cable and sank her teeth into the steel. The oily water closed over the last of the wharves. Her mission was completed.

Through a little window in the wrist of her black rubber frogwoman's suit she saw that it was only two hours since she had left the Colonel's office. She felt her way through the dark hut to the doorway, and out into the chill, mountain air. She carefully adjusted her skates, pulled out from the kerb and made for the centre-line of the road.

She smiled gently in the darkness, and switched on her tail-light. It was, she thought as she spat out a few shreds of cable, good—she paused and lit a cigar—to be—as James would say—alive.

Soup-marked Money: The language of prices of goods sold in a soup-marked, or self-service grocery. The following are typical examples: fawn ten; fawn tum sipenee; nime-pen soff; sick snite; tairmpen soff; tumce, etc. These terms are of particular interest to the historian, as they will disappear with the introduction of dismal guernsey, after which time all prices will be expressed in dolls and sense.

Spargly Guys: *see* Tiger.

Spin-ear Mitch: Much alike; closely resembling one another. As in: 'He's the spin-ear mitch of his old man.'

Split Nair Dyke: A continual sensation of pain in the head. As in: 'I got a split nair dyke. Smor niken bear; I left a tiger nipey sea.'

Spoultered: *see* Gunga Din.

Star Ginter: *see* Stark Ender.

Stark Ender: (Or, occasionally, Star Ginter.) An enthusiastic attack. As in: 'They all got stark ender the grog on Ear's Eve.'

Stewnce: Persons engaged in learning something from books, or attending an educational institution, especially of the higher class; scholars; persons dedicated to the pursuit of knowledge. As in: Four stewnce were arrested and charged with offensive behaviour. Or: Plea sledge stewnce threw Exeter bystanner.

Swice, Swy: So I. As in: 'Swice settwer wine chermine cherrone business, I settwer snunner your business wad-eye do.' or: 'Swy roe twim an I toldim jus wad-eye thorter fim. Oy's a sarder sniles.'

Tan Cancel: The elected local government authority.

Tea Nature: *see* Girldie Larks.

Teedo, Dorimy Fasola: World-famous lyricist and soprano. Strines have every reason to be proud of the many famous singers their country has produced—Joe Nammon, Nellie Mairlper, Peer Torzen, Joan Sullon and, above all, the glorious Dorimy Fasola Teedo, whose name will forever be graven on the hearts of all true Strines. Madame Teedo—known to all her adorers as the Mordialloc Magpie — is unique in Strine musical history. Her golden voice and tempestuous personality are indeed legendary, but it is as a lyricist and composer that her true brilliance is revealed. Perhaps the best-loved of her perennially popular songs are 'There are Ferries at the Bomb of my Garden', and 'Dicey, Dicey, Give me your Ant, Sir, Do!' Another favourite, 'La, Fizzer Mannie's Planet—Think' has been translated into 53 languages. Even in the most remote parts of Norn Tare Tree and Vitamin Bay one may hear the natives singing, in their quaint accents, the well-known words of this moving ballad which has here been translated as 'Love is Money Splattered Thick'.

Temps: *see* Harps.

Term Night Sear: Terminates here. (*See also* Rye-Wye.)

Terror Souse: One of a number of conjoined double- or triple-storeyed dwellings found in older parts of some capital cities (Fissroy, Paddo, North Air Delight, etc.). Antonym: Gloria Soame (*q.v.*).

We have bought ourselves a terror souse in Paddo
In a district which is squalid but admired.
It's a pity that the rooms are full of shadow,
And the bathroom leaves so much to be desired.

Of course we had to spend a bit of money;
The plumbing was, well—you know, rather quaint.
We live mostly in the kitchen where it's sunny.
(It's wonderful what you can do with paint.)

Our neighbours are artistic and they love us.
(The ironwork, though meagre, is a dream.)
A 'thing' lives in the attic up above us.
We haven't seen it yet—just heard it scream.

Tiger: Imperative mood of the verb to take. As in: 'Tiger look at this, Reg, you wooden reader battit', or 'Tiger perrer spargly guys.'

Titch, Gloria Sarah: Madame Titch is perhaps even more revered than Ned Kelly or the bellicose but lovable War Sigma Tilda. Gloria Sarah Titch has always been a great favourite of Strine elder statesmen, who often refer to her in their more exuberant exhortations,

But hula calf
trim
Y. limer Y?
Summon scotter look
calf trim.
Summer nester
Phillip E. Sworter
and gimmies
tier nawl

Nair
dent-shoe worry.
Iler calf trim.
Sleece tiger do.
Watsy effris tea?
Dar sneff
March dussy?
Undersea
effny think frizz
breckfuss?

e.g. 'This is our Gloria Sarah Titch—we must defend it with your last drop of blood!' or 'If you vote for those dingoes you'll be betraying our Gloria Sarah Titch.'

To Gorf: To leave suddenly; to begin flying. As in: 'He to gorf like a rocket'; 'He to gorf like a batter to hell'. Antonym: To lairnd. As in: 'He to gorf at tempest four, Annie lairnded a Tairsenden atterbat harps nine.'

Trine: *see* Rye-Wye.

Uppendan: To and fro; backwards and forwards. As in: 'She walked uppendan Flinner Street farairs, an then she finey got a cabbome to Cannerbry.'

Utter Martyr: *see* Semmitch.

Wairtsed: *see* Jareedna.

Weird: Electric railway station near Hunner Street, Sinny. Trines leave Weird for Naw Sinny, Slennets and the Naw Shaw. (*See also* Naw Shaw; and Rye-Wye.) Note: Weird should not be confused with the English word *weird*, as in *They're a Weird Mob*.

Wezzme: Where is my. As in: 'Wezzme hembairg and wezzme earniform?' or 'Wezzme pressure-pack sherry and meem rangs an me autographed photo of Lassie?'

Wisperoo Des: A noted name in Strine literature. Notorious for his harshness, hated by the prisoners, feared by man and animal alike, Wisperoo Des is the brutal main character in the long epic poem, 'Chris and Des' by Adam Lizzie Gorn. The following oft-quoted passage is from the famous duel scene in Act IV:

(*Enter, Ned Kelly, carrying easel, brushes and several 44-gallon drums of synthetic enamel. Offstage, sounds of critics clicking ball-point pens.*)

Kelly: Harsh, harsh Wisperoo Des
And Chrissofer Robin have fallen danstairs.
Anorlerking sauces anorlerking smen
Are watching the mares and the birdies again.

Would never: Do not have. As in: 'You would never
light wood-germite?' or 'Ar would never glue.'

X: The twenty-fourth letter of the Strine alphabet; also
plural of egg; also a tool for chopping wood.

Yeggowan: Do you intend travelling to? As in: 'Yeggowan Rare Wick Sairdy?' or 'Yeggowan E. Smelpen
on Wensdy? Ora yeggowan togota Sunkilta?'

Zarf Trawl: Because after all. As in: 'Zarf trawl Leica
nony doomy Bess.' or: 'Zarf trawl wee rony flesh and
blood wennit Saul boiled down.'

NOSE TONE UNTURNED

NOSE TONE UNTURNED

People, predicaments and poems

CONTENTS

ACKNOWLEDGEMENTS

The author expresses his grateful acknowledgements to the *Sydney Morning Herald,* in which much of the material in this book originally appeared. He also expresses his gratitude to the many hundreds of correspondents who have so kindly offered him advice and information about obscure Strine words and phrases. He regret that he has been unable to answer all these letters individually, and takes this opportunity of saying — Thank you.

He would also like to express his warmest thanks to the following people for their help in a variety of ways:

To A.T.B. for his continued invaluable criticism and advice;

To Judy Burns for permission to reproduce the music she wrote for Tim Pannelli's song;

To his assistant, Andrew Paragon, for his never-failing tolerance and patience;

To his secretary, Philippa Nibbly, for bringing, to page 107, only one of those sandwiches; and also for chair kinny spairlin;

And, finally, to Alistair Morrison, without whose help this book would never have been completed.

FOREWORD

I met Afferbeck Lauder for the first time many years ago, when he was staying in the house with my family. Then, of course, I didn't know his name — this was to be a fairly recent discovery. He was always, though you may now find this almost incredible, a shy, retiring sort of a fellow. Brilliant, of course — at least I always found him so, and with a keen ear for the nuances of the language, I enjoyed his company more than most people's, and I certainly laughed at his wit more than at anyone else's. We were inseparable companions, and so I came to know him extraordinarily intimately; indeed he became almost a sort of *alter ego*. For some reason he always shunned the public gaze. He even went so far as to adopt various disguises from time to time; which gave us both a great deal of wry amusement. It was only after the publication of *Let Stalk Strine* that I was able to prevail upon him to come out into the open — to accept his mantle of fame.

This new publication, which has given me enormous pleasure, brings you a more complete picture of the man than his previous work, crammed as it was with hard facts, could possibly have done. I hope you all enjoy it even half as much as I have.

Sydney, 1966   ALISTAIR MORRISON

A DAY AT THE BIG STORE

'He who enters shop with lady or davvy zed-red' — Strine
proverb

When I entered Suite 307 on the third floor of the Hotel
Magna I was only mildly dismayed and not really at all
surprised to find a rather patient-looking gorilla poring
over some papers at the desk, and a large albino aardvark
sitting on the bed, wearing an ill-fitting yellow wig, and
sawing the tips off her claws — or perhaps she was painting
her nails; I couldn't be sure which. It had, after all, been a
morning of one extraordinary incident after another, and
by now I was almost completely unflabbergastable.

What had happened was that, earlier, as I was walking
to the bus, I had encountered a small boy on a surfskate —
or rather he had encountered me. He had zoomed past me
downhill on his way to the gum-vending machine, and had
joggled me and screeched *'Ny'anng!'* into my good ear,
giving me such a fright that I had jumped about two feet
into the sky and had dropped my bifocals irretrievably
down a stormwater grating. Since then I had, in my half
blind state, been involved in a series of most disconcerting
confrontations. I had raised my hat in polite greeting to a
neighbour, and had said, 'Good morning, Mrs Kratchnoff.
How are you, and how's Ron? How did the budgies like
the kelp?' and had been shocked by her deep bass reply,
'Listen, mate, knock it off will you or I'll call the troopers.'
The bus conductor had refused my fare because he was in
fact a fireman, and the hairless and pitifully shrunken old

woman to whom I gave my seat had waved a black snake at me and said, 'Goo!' several times before I discovered that she was a toddler with a licorice strap. And so it had continued the whole morning. How could I now be worried by such small-time stuff as a poring gorilla and a sawing aardvark?

The gorilla got up from the desk and shook my hand, 'Ah, Afferbeck. Nice to see you.' The aardvark stopped hacking her extremities, and smirked at me and said, 'Smf!' and I knew then that I was in the right room. It was clear now that the gorilla was not only human but was also my old friend Dr Willi Schkrambl of the Polyglot Institute at Grinzing. The aardvark was of course Madame Schkrambl. I'd made no mistake about the wig though — it *was* a wig; her usual ill-fitting yellow one, through which she now ran her fingers, shaking her head back with a typically masculine flourish.

Dr Schkrambl, an anthropologist of considerable renown, had come to Australia to study some of the more obscure customs of the inhabitants, and to investigate and to record for his institute the intricate subtleties of the Strine language. Naturally I had offered to help in any way I could, and so here I was, for the twentieth day in succession, escorting him and his aardvark wife on a tour of local oddities. I had thought, when I first offered my services, that the whole operation would be a pushover, but I hadn't taken into account Madame Schkrambl's extraordinary energy and perseverance. She was indefatigable — I am not. My spirit is willing but my feet are weak.

I apologized for being late. After the usual shuffling around and talking about the weather Madame Schkrambl made it clear to me, by means of eye-rolling, sign language, and what she thought was English, that we were today going on a tour of department stores. 'Oh no! Not that!' I heard my feet say. Her husband said he thought it would be a good opportunity to hear some specialized Strine. I don't think really that he had any part in the decision, but he always put on a convincing show of strength.

'Yuiff snar. Gsengel — so!' said Madame Schkrambl. As usual I didn't know what she was talking about but I could see, even in my monofocal, presbyopic condition, that she was hopping with restlessness, so, without further discussion, we took off.

'. . . dress material spiper pairten slidy snitwear all kiddieswear corsetry cropperdy travel good slidy sarnderwear maternity boutique and souvenirs goer *nar* please!' said the lift driver.

'Pliz klu — slom!' said Madame Schkrambl as we emerged onto the field of battle. She pointed a trembling finger at a sign which read: Budgetwear for the Mature Figure. Her eyes rolled with excitement, and her nostrils dilated so that she looked like a rocking mare. 'Pliz translite,' she said with husky joy.

'It says: Expensive clothes for fat old women,' I told her, but already she was in a semi-trance.

'Lesker datter this quick,' said Dr Schkrambl, justifiably panic-stricken, but determined, as usual, to speak Strine whenever possible. 'Lesker danter the tool snardware,' he continued, 'Ah wanner gessem Sam Piper n' turps.' But he was too late — much too late; Madame Schkrambl was already almost out of eye-shot, burrowing into the budgetwear with a saleswoman who had appeared, like a bush fly, suddenly from nowhere.

Dr Schkrambl tried again. 'Gretlklein, lesker datter this, *dear* . . .' he shouted, his cupped hands to his mouth. But it was hopeless. We looked at each other. 'About an hour, I would think, wouldn't you?' I said.

'Yair, batter narret least,' he answered with resignation, 'Or nairer nar feven. Ware, lesket bacter work. You ready?' He sat down on the floor with his back against a display of drastically reduced imported famous-name knitwear oddments many below cost, and motioned to me to sit down beside him. He took out a notebook and pencil, and fingered his way down the pages.

'Yair, seewee are,' he said. 'Hisswear we leftorf at the concert la snite. Now — what's the English for: I rare jaw la spook — reel good. Air nephew ritter nennie moorpook slightly?'

'In English,' I told him, 'you'd say: I read your last book and found it quite entertaining. And do you expect to have anything new published in the near future?' He noted all this down carefully.

'Now, bairns?' he asked, 'Bairns are what you call kiddies, I suppose? Same as in Scotland.'

'Oh no,' I corrected him, 'Bairns are either musical groups — you know like chairs bairns — or else they can be — ah, sort of loops, like rubber bairns. You remember the line: The mussel zonny sprawny arm stuttairt li-gine bairns.'

'I see, I see. Well now . . .' he consulted his notebook. 'What about Hazzy? This means: Has he?'

'No, hazzy means: How is he? As in: Hazzy gairt nonnets cool? or: Hazzy gairt non wither mare thorgon?'

'Ah, good. Now, what's machewer mean?'

'Machoor,' I corrected his pronunciation. 'Machoor means: ripe; fully developed; experienced. For example, you'd say: Listen, chicken, what mortgage you want thanner machoor manner the world like me? Although, strictly speaking, when you address a lady as chicken, it is more correct to say machoor rooster of the world.'

'Ah, so! Machoor rooster. Reel good.' He made copious notes. I remembered that he had always taken a keen interest in birds, and was in fact president of the Grinzing branch of Voluptuaries Anonymous.

'So!' He nodded his head several times with satisfaction. 'And now,' he continued, 'Here's one which has puzzled me. What's Dopey's prize? A consolation prize perhaps?'

'Oh no, Dopey's prize is a sort of warning, as in: Okay, go ahead and bitey zearoff, but dopey's prize diffy bite spak; arf trawly zony human.'

'Ah, good, good. Well now, what's a knotter fiker?'

I peered at the budgetwear to see what was going on. They were apparently still engaged in the preliminaries; not even at the trying-on stage yet. I was getting hungry. I had a headache from the effort of surviving in a hostile environment without bifocals. I knew that before the day was over we would have walked through miles of department store, and that I would be suffering the agonies of British Museum feet. I forced myself to attend to what my companion had been saying.

'Knotter fiker?' I said, 'Well, that's incomplete really. It is usually followed by some such word as nairlpit. For instance, you'd say — or I would, anyway, that's for sure: We woker meara gain. Knotter fiker nairlpit.'

In the distance I could see Madame Schkrambl and the bush fly lady disappearing into the trying-on rooms, each carrying about a dozen multicoloured machoor figure jobs. Dr Schkrambl sighed patiently. He shut his notebook and put it back in his pocket. 'Ware lider nair bare chew,' he said, 'but I mungry. Hair batter cabbage Eno — Anna bitter G. Skite?' He poke Strine like a native — a remarkable achievement.

HAGGER NIGH TELL?

Hagger nigh telephime reely reel?
Hadder Y. Noah Fimere?
Car sigh ony nowered I thing ky feel,
An maybe I'm knotty veneer.

I mipey no lesson I mipey no more
Than a shadder we idle fancy.
Prabzyme the moon! Can I Telfer Shaw
That I'm nodgers a nant named Nancy?

I coobie jar sreely a loafer bread,
Or a horse, or a bird called Gloria.
I mipey alive — but I coobie dead,
Or a phantasmabloodygoria.

Hagger nigh tellime notonia dream,
Cook tarpner mare chick's pell?
Cor sigh my pig zackly what I seem,
Bar towg nigh reely tell?

.   .   .   .   .

Wunker nawlwye stell; yegger nawlwye snow
If you're reelor yerony dreaming;
Yellopoff the topoff your nirra stow,
A new wafer the sander the screaming.

THE GENTLEST MAN

I arrived at the airport with time to spare. It was cold, and I stood near one of the heaters while I waited for the big jet to arrive.

I took out Geoffrey's letter and read it again. He would be in Australia for a few days, he had written, before going on to Melbourne (typical), and he was looking forward to seeing me. He was preparing a paper on semantics, which he was to read to some egghead show or other he'd been made a fellow of. And what did I think of the title? 'Mystery Lingo Bid Baffles Euroglots.' He wanted to include some examples of Strine and other obscure (!) languages. He had heard of my appointment to the post of Professor of Strine Studies at the University of Sinny, and could I give him an hour or so on such and such a date? And he was mine sincerely, Geoffrey.

Obscure indeed! How like him. Anything he didn't know much about was obscure. He probably even thought Australia was an English-speaking country; he was incredibly ignorant. Still, he was a nice fellow; kind and gentle.

I looked at my watch. The plane was late. I wandered over to the newsstand and looked at the near-naked girls on the magazine covers. Pretty girls they were, too. One, I noticed, a particularly robust type, proudly overtopping her skimpy bra, bore the legend: Two Big Lift-outs. My mind started to wander along a warm, familiar track, when, suddenly — it happened!

Paaaaaaaaaaahr! Graggle! Tzinggggggg! Pikpik! An appalling noise, practically inside my head. I was standing immediately below one of the public address outlets.

This sort of thing is always happening to me. Just thinking about something, quietly minding my own business, and suddenly — Peng! Someone runs into me on a bicycle, or something blows up in my face. James Bond never goes on like this; why do I? Absent-minded I suppose. The absent-minded professor. James Bond! I wondered if Geoffrey was a spy. Perhaps he was really coming out here to ask me. . . .

Poong! Grag grag! Aaaaaaaa-pik! I jumped again, but only a few inches this time. *Yorred hessian plaize. Flight glargle glargle glar Baggokokko Sicker Paw nair riving ahpem ah-pem ah-pem. Pik!* Well, here it was. I moved over to where the crowd had gathered, and waited for him to come through the Customs.

I went forward with my hand out, to greet him, but he never saw me — just stared right through me, looking for someone. Me, I suppose. I had to grab his arm.

'Airfferbairk! My dear chairp!' He beamed at me with pleasure. 'Dewno I dint even nerr you.'

'I've had my hair cut shorter,' I said.

'No, no, old chairp. It's because you look sirmer cholder.'

He always was completely truthful; I can't imagine how he had managed to last so long on a newspaper. Still, he didn't have to be quite so brutal.

Eventually I got him settled into his hotel. We sat down in his suite and had tea and sandwiches. Then he took out a very small notebook and a silver pencil about the size of a match. He looked at me indulgently, a gentle smile on his happy, foolish face, and said, glancing at his very thin watch, 'Airps-loo-lair marfless to see you, old chairp. Now I've got about twenty minutes. Tell me airfrithing about Strine.'

Everything! Twenty minutes! After thirty years of research!

'Snow datter batcher, yerron yerrone,' I said, and watched him blink.

'What's that, old chairp?'

'Snore flotta effter tellion lesser narfer nair.'

He stopped smiling, and opened and shut his mouth a few times. 'Liss-nole chairp, do talk English.' He leant forward and patted my hand gently.

'Ah-na, Chair-free, jar slesky pon torgon Strine,' I said.

He put down his notebook and pencil. Then he got through to room service and ordered a bottle of scotch.

'Answer mice,' I said.

'And some ice,' he repeated. He didn't say anything more until we each had a drink in front of us. Then all he said was, 'Ah!'

'Tell me, Geoffrey,' I said, 'This work you're doing. Marspy ferry in a resting.' He just stared at me with his mouth open. The time had come to stop matter-mincing.

'Look, Geoffrey, don't you realise this is a foreign country? You can't talk English all the time as though you were in Dijon, or Gothenburg, or Zurich or somewhere. You're in Australia now, not Europe, and if you want to get anywhere you'll have to learn the language. And it'll certainly take you more than twenty minutes.'

'Yes, old chairp. I see that now. I hadn't realized. Vair good of you to make it so clear.' He was so subdued now that I felt sorry for him, and a little ashamed. After all, he was such a nice, gentle fellow, really.

'Now look Geoff,' I said, 'we haven't got much time. So let's take a few simple phrases — the sort of thing you'll need to get you through the next few days. There won't be time for nice distinctions, and cosy, finical hoo-ha. Just the rough stuff. You mightn't like this way of learning a language, but, well, yell jess tefter get chews twit.'

He sat up straight. 'I'll have to get what?'

'Chews twit,' I repeated, 'Youlga chews twit!'

He started to smile. 'Chews twit. Yes, I see. Get chews

twit. Arlga chews twit. How's that?' He waited anxiously for praise.

'Very good indeed,' I said. 'Excellent. Now what's this I'm holding up?'

'A plastic raincoat, of course.'

'No, try again.'

He moved his lips around, silently. I watched his silly face light up.

'A plair stig rairn court?'

'No, no. Nottingham, perhaps. Or Dublin or somewhere. But not Strine. Pleh. Pleh . . .' I prompted him, coaxed him, and finally he got it.

'A plesty crine coat, a plesty crine coat, a plesty bloody crinecoat.' He was grinning now, and somehow looked harder, and tougher. He made an odd sort of movement, and for a moment I thought he was going to spit on the floor.

'Well now,' I continued, 'let's take a typical, everyday situation. The sort of thing that's bound to happen if you're going to be here for a few days. Yes, I know. Say you're travelling in a suburban train. A young man gets in and sits beside you. He pulls out a flick-knife and starts slashing at the upholstery. Now what do you do?'

'I'd say to him, Now look here, old chairp. No, that can't be right. No, I don't really know what I'd do. I give up; what should I say to the fellow?'

'Well, to begin with, you don't *say* anything. What you have to *do* is — now, are you ready? Wait for it — you kingie minner teeth!'

'I kingie minner teeth. I kingie minner teeth!' he shouted with delight. He punched his right fist into his left palm, and spat on the floor. 'I kingie minner teeth! I kingie minner teeth, inner teeth, inner teeth, TEETH!' He couldn't stop. He was jumping up and down, his face transformed. 'I kingie minner teeth! I kingie minner teeth agair, nanna, gair nanna, GAIRN!'

A little line of saliva ran down from one corner of his mouth. It was frightening. I was beginning to feel as a psychiatrist must feel when he has dug too deep, too quickly, and has hit something. I hoped I hadn't created a Frankenstrine monster.

I tried to calm him by talking English, but it didn't work.

'Take it easy,' I said. But perhaps he didn't understand English any more.

'Yuma sketcher cell farner control. Try talking English. You know — English?'

'Snow ewe smite,' he said, 'I've gedadda the wire-fit.' He had me really worried now. Would I have to give him largactil to terminate it? He was worried too, apparently, very worried.

'Arkahn's top! Warm-eye gonadoo? Hair my gona gedadda this?'

'Take it easy, Geoff. Take it easy.'

'Tiger teasie, tiger teasie. Saul-wright few!' He was in a panic now, giving little low moans, and kicking a pillow around the room, screaming, 'Kingie minner teeth, the drongo!' Then he started to cry. He picked up the bible from the bedside table, and got down on his knees. 'Matthew, Ma, Kloogenjahn! Oh, parrot I slossed! Oh, Lord, mike me a pommagairn. I wonna go woam. I wommy mummy. I dough wonnerby star gear frevver.' He was wailing wildly and tearing at his forearms. There was no time now to get help. No time for doctors with needles. There was only one thing to do. I picked up the whisky bottle, and let him have it — right onny zoxyput!

I got him onto the bed, and covered him up with a blanket. He'd just have to sleep it off. I hoped he *would* sleep it off. I sat down and waited. No point in getting anyone else in, until I saw how he was when he came to. I'd have to be very careful not to speak anything but English. Someone else might easily say something like, 'Prab zeiche nelpew', and he'd be off again. I sat back and waited.

Gradually he began to look a little better; a little bit less like Jekyll and Hyde, and a bit more like his usual self — like Laurel and Hardy.

About an hour later he stirred and opened his eyes. I waited anxiously for his first words. He sat up, very slowly. 'King . . . King . . .' he said. I reached for the bottle, but he lay down again. Then he sat up once more. 'King. King. I say, old chairp, I've had a very odd dream. Something about teeth. Very odd.' He looked puzzled. 'I say, old chairp, what happened?'

I was so relieved I nearly cried. Too relieved, really; I relaxed and, without thinking, said, 'You got star ginter the turp smite.' However, nothing happened; he just looked more puzzled than ever.

'I must have had a drop too much. Joy good of you to look after me, old chairp. What's happened to my head?'

'There it is. Look — on your neck. Take it out and put it under the tap for a while.'

He got up and had a shower, and in about half an hour he seemed perfectly all right, and was asking me about the Strine language, and could I give him an hour or so to-morrow? I said I'd have to check with my secretary.

He thanked me again for being so kind. He couldn't understand how it had happened. I explained that the scotch had been bottled in Australia, and so it was much stronger than anything he'd get at home. It seemed to satisfy him.

By the time I left he was whistling softly, and saying 'King king king' gently to himself. But then he does everything gently. The gentlest man I've ever known — I think.

THE BOSSA NYE

Ware niker tinter work now
The bossa zinner hedomy;
Ickisser smee, and sair, 'Swill yubie mine?'
I got a rillked lurk now;
'I lar few, dear,' he sedomy,
But ice air, 'Gee, it sneely ah-pa snine.'

. . . . . .

I fleft me jobber twirk now;
The bosket spy withairt me;
A niken stayer tome a slardger slife.
I give a little smirk now;
The bossle torga bairt me:
'Me sekkertry has nowbie cummy wife.'

BIG DEAL WITH MISS HIGHWATER

A few days ago I was sitting at my desk, in a semi-coma-tose condition, trying, without much success, to digest one of those meals for which the staff canteen is famous all over Australia and the South Pacific area. Spaghetti and baked beans on toast with mashed potatoes had been fol-lowed by something which on Mondays, Wednesdays and Fridays is known as Cabinet Pudding, and on Tuesdays and Thursdays as Spotted Dog. All this had been ade-quately irrigated with semi-opaque tea from a monolithic, lolly-pink cup.

I remembered having been informed years ago, by an advertisement, that the acid in my stomach would burn a hole in the carpet. I now appreciated the undeniable truth of this majestic statement. I helped myself to still another spoonful of sodium bicarbonate from a jar which I keep suspended from the ceiling on a length of string, and called to my secretary in the next room.

'Miss Nibbly, kannewka minneara minute?' I find I nearly always speak Strine in moments of anguish or dis-may.

Miss Nibbly came running, eyebrows raised.

'Air you all rate, professor? Orv you bin lenching et the centeen again?'

'Miss Nibbly,' I said, 'I have a premonition that some-thing terrible is about to happen.' I looked down to see if any holes were appearing in the carpet yet.

She looked at her watch. 'York weight rate, professor. Miss Highwater is coming to do you et three.'

Suddenly it all came back to me, bringing with it a sink-ing feeling in the pit of what was once my stomach. Good heavens! Helen Highwater — and no place to hide.

This internationally famous journalist had telephoned earlier in the week to say that she would like to 'do' me in the weekly women's journal which she edits. Obviously she was hoping to increase her own apparent intellectual stature by having me appear in her lousy journal, but what could I do? I abhor the limelight, but I had to consider the interests of the University; after all *Womb and Sty* has an enormous circulation. And so I had agreed. 'Don't forget to bring a photographer,' I had said.

And now she would be here any minute. I straightened my collar, brushed away a few traces of spotted dog, and started to look distinguished. I could hear an increasing commotion in the outer office. She had arrived.

'My dear Helen.' I rose and greeted her. 'How nice to see you.'

This was not, strictly speaking, true; it wasn't nice to see her at all. She is a noisy, over-emphatic woman in her late fifties. She was wearing, as usual, a face such as one ordinarily wouldn't expect to see outside a zoo.

'Afferbeck, dear boy,' she trumpeted, 'How are you?' Involuntarily, I glanced up to see if the mahout was there, sitting on her head.

'Not bad, Helen. . . .' I started to tell her about my indigestion, hoping to follow up with details of recent visits from various viruses. Then I planned to touch lightly on the more popular, semi-chronic items like slipped disc and insomnia. But I could see that she was fidgeting, and had disconnected her hearing aid. This is what is so maddening about the woman — asks you a question, and then doesn't listen to the answer.

She had settled herself in a chair and was scratching around in a large handbag, from which she now extracted a notebook the size of a ledger. She reconnected her hearing aid and lit a cigarette. I cleared my throat.

'Well,' I said, 'I assume that your readers will want to know all the usual things. My background and qualifications, and so on. Then, I suppose, a few comments about my next book; my plans for the future. Perhaps a few paragraphs about my philosophy of life. A brisk run through the wife and kiddies; and how I first became interested in the Strine language. That should about cover it, don't you think?'

'Of course, dear boy,' she replied. 'But there's a little matter I'd like to discuss with you first.' She tore two or three pages out of the ledger, folded them in half, and sat on them. 'As you know,' she went on, 'I've just returned from a journey all over Australia by bicycle. Well, of course, I met and talked with all kinds of people. Desert tribesmen, housewives, truckies, bush nurses, doggers, hatters, shearers, swaggies, opal miners, rabbiters, lurk men, lubras, and doctors — both Flying and witch.' She paused, and smiled her crinkly, moon-faced smile.

'I thought of you, dear boy,' she went on. 'And I collected for you a dozen or more quite rare Strine words and phrases. I'm sure most of them will be new to you.'

So that's how the old bag got those billiard-table legs — pedalling about the hinterland on a two-wheeler. Still, it was good of her to think of my interests in this way.

'That's extraordinarily kind of you, Helen,' I said, leaning across and patting what I thought was probably a knee. I held out my hand for the loot.

'Just a moment, dear boy,' she said. 'These are valuable.'

I didn't catch on at first. Then, suddenly, I saw what she meant. The old camel wanted to *sell* them to me. I was horrified. I stalled for time. I went over to the window and swatted a few dreamy blowflies. I bit a few fingernails. I got out the polish and started to clean my shoes. I mustn't seem too anxious. I went back slowly, and sat down again.

'You must be joking, of course, Helen. But then you always were a remarkably witty woman.

'I said they're valuable,' she repeated. She was now clutching the pages in her mighty fist.

What could I do? I had to have them, but I couldn't let her know this. What was my next move to be? I couldn't just say — How much?

'How much?' I said.

'Fifty dollars a word,' she replied, without hesitation.

'You're mad, you hideous old dragon!' I shouted at her with icy dignity, dancing up and down.

'First of all, dear boy, don't call me old. And secondly, if you don't want them I'll let the Rockefeller Foundation have them, they've already made me an offer.'

Good heavens! This was appalling. I'd be the laughing stock of the academic world if anyone published them before I did — this was my subject. She was probably bluffing, but I couldn't take any risks. I must remain quite calm. I banged on the desk with both fists, as imperturbable as ever.

'Listen to me, you fiendish old trombone,' I screeched at her. 'Where do you think I'm going to get that sort of money? I'll give you twenty dollars each. How many are there?'

'Oooo — about a dozen or so. No, dear boy, not a cent less than fifty dollars.'

A dozen! At fifty dollars! I called out to my assistant, Dr Paragon, and asked him to work it out for me. I finished polishing my shoes while I waited.

Eventually, slide rule in hand, he came in with the answer — seven hundred and forty seven dollars!

'Seffer narnet and voice airven.' I broke into Strine in my anguish. 'Why couldn't you have left me alone with my stomach, you web-footed old bat? I was happy before you came. And how do I know you're not conning me? You old slug; you ought to be pole-axed. How about a free sample?'

'Okay,' she agreed, after some hesitation, 'One free

sample, with translation, and two without.' She peered down at the pages, 'Soym Gwynn,' she said at last, 'Soym Gwynn. That's a very rare one. I got it from a pearl diver up near Broome. Cost me a packet, too. He was telling me about the time his First Engineer was drowned in the Coral Sea. I soym gwynn, he said to me, butter dinsim carmairt. Northern Strine, very valuable.' She smiled happily as she ran a horny finger down the page, looking for goodies.

'And how about these?' she went on. 'Arlu clugger, and dokey ponner. I tell you, dear boy, you're getting them cheap. And here's a song about Y. Lezzer Kahn. Oooo, and at least a dozen more, accurately translated and copiously annotated.'

I was shaking with excitement. What could an arlu clugger be? Who was Y. Lezzer Kahn, that they should have felt impelled to write a song about him? What was a dokey ponner — animal, vegetable or mineral?

'Forty dollars?' I said. But I knew it was a waste of time; my trembling hands gave me away.

'Listen, dear boy, I said fifty — and I meant it. Now hurry, I mustn't be late for the Prime Minister.'

I reached for my cheque book. My capitulation was complete.

'How do you spell your name, Helen? With one scream or two?' I made out the cheque for a hundred and fifty dollars, and borrowed the rest from petty cash.

She handed me the pages. I went out with her and helped her onto her bicycle, and pushed her off down the hill. I ran back to my office, sick with excitement. Arlu clugger! Y. Lezzer Whatsisname! I rubbed my sweating hands with joy.

I locked the door, and opened up my prize. Nice, neat handwriting, too. Good old Helen, always so reliable.

Dokey ponner (I read): meaning, Please stop reminding me. As in: Okay, okay, I said I was sorry. Jars dokey ponner battered. Source: A psychiatrist at Lightning

Ridge, scolded by his wife for having put largactil in her lolly-water.

Arlu clugger: I resemble. As in: Arno arlu clugger nairedale, buttem rilly a border collie. Source: A sheep dog called Caliban, at Peak Hill, New South Wales.

Pidiot Stoo: It is unfortunate that it is too. . . . As in: Pidiot stoo early flunch. Canniver bitter bren jairm? Source: A ten year old hyperthyroid bread and jam addict, son of a Rockhampton cane-cutter.

Y. Lezzer Kahn: Character in the song, *The Law Y. Spear Ningland Y. Lezzer Kahn Treeline*. Source: The occasion of an evening party after the picnic races at Gooblawookla, near Eucla. We all sat around the campfire, and sang all the old favourites, *The Law Y. Spear Ningland, Long Wider Tier Prairie,* and *Arse Wheat Miss Drear Flife*.

I ran my eyes over the lovely lovely list. Thaw ninny side; Fordyce and Fawnite Sweek; noker parison; umpziggen tardafit; Theng Q. Bubbeye; Karkasova chicken; how swarming; the Serviette Union; far spola; Hymen Island; snow trarpler tall; ease dregs; gun cedar woofer the trees; Noah to park; the dotted lion; welker mome; wee jar stono; mife yon say; sloombar. . . .

And about a dozen more. I'd certainly got my money's worth. Perhaps she'd given me some of the Prime Minister's too, by mistake. What a bargain! Only seven hundred and something dollars. Why, they'd have cost me twice that on the black market. Good old Helen. An attractive woman too, in a repellent sort of way.

LA DOLCE VITA

I think that I shall never see
A treer sluffly yazzer poem.
The cool fresh water snoffer me,
But champagne by the jeroboam.

I got no time for lousy trees,
Withaw lem leaves an birds an nests;
The darling starling isstomy
The dreariest of lousy pests.

Gimme the brighter sneon lights;
The laugh teroff the dancing girls,
With mini-skirts an lacy tights,
An stardust in their lacquered curls.

Gimme a car with plennier power,
An gimmier drinker tenny cost.
This is my finest, final hour;
I mitching to be level-crossed.

BRA SHARP YOUR STRINE

Calm nodomy a gine, but cider Airthens,
Timer nath mighty zephyr-lasting mention
A ponner beached verger the salt flar,
Do once a die withis embossed froth
The turbulent surchall carver; thither Carmen,
Lep-mye grive's tone be or Rorricle:
Lips, lets air word skobyen, Lang gwichairnd:
Wadders a miss, Ply gannon Fection mairnd.
Grive zony bee-men's work, san Death air gine;
Saar, nide thy beams, Timer nath dunny's Rhine.

Few occupations are more rewarding, more deeply satisfy-
ing, than translating Shakespeare into Strine. I had already
completed *Hairmlet* and *A Winner Style,* and now, at last,
here I was almost at the end of *Time Honour Vairthens.*
I would have given anything to be able, now, to start on
Macbeth. Of course I still had a few senatorial loose ends
to clear up with Timon; Alcibiades and the epitaph and
everything. But these could wait; Macbeth was calling me,
clamouring to be done into Strine — the noblest language
of them all. But more pressing things were at hand. Reluc-
tantly I put Timon aside; with a sigh I dismissed Macbeth.
It was time for the half-yearly examination of the second-
year students. I called Miss Nibbly and asked her to give
me the final draft of the paper I had prepared.

I read it through carefully. Not bad — not bad at all
really. I had thought that I would need to do some more
work on it, but no, it seemed okay. Comprehensive, varied,

not too difficult and yet not too obviously a pushover. I decided to let it go as it was. I corrected the spelling of the word *earmile,* and asked Miss Nibbly to run off the usual number of copies. Then I locked the door and drew the curtains. I took down Macbeth. At last, at last! Meanwhile, Miss Nibbly was hard at work.

STRINE II — Half-yearly Examination.
(Possible marks: 100)

(1) Who are Arch and T. Nairns? Where are Lucas Heights and Fagger's Heights? What is the meaning of: A Skymer Snairk Ellie? (5 marks)

(2) Translate the following into English:
She scone orphan tyken the kiddie swither; He nair fradder penny Toohey snime; Chew plonker the bowling clarp? (5 marks)

(3) Write twenty-five words in Strine about any three of the following:
Phenobarbecuticle; Leprecapricornucopia; Earmile and Surfer Smile; The Flying Sorceress of Bonnie Doom. (5 marks)

(4) Compose a telegram of seventy to a hundred words, and include as many as possible of the following Strine words:
Ice-cream; flake; dim; choir; Carmen; cauliflowers; doubt; crairnonnie; try; low; sawn-off; butcher; dough; rand; loafer; sighed; sneck; eyesore; craw; dadda; zed; sore; lassie.
The following is given as an example of the sort of thing that is required. However you are expected to use your own imagination, and not merely to copy or rearrange.

EYESORE A BIG DOG CARMEN AWARDS ME IT
WAS A CAULI FLOWERS WERE A RAND E SNECK
ANDY WORE A CRAIRNONNIE ZED GOLLY ITSA
CAULI ICE-HEAD IT LOOKS LIKE SAWN-OFF
LASSIE OR RIN TIN TINNERS CHOIR I PADDER
DIM ON THE CROWN BUT HE LOOKED CRAW
SIGHED AT ME AND SAID DOUGH BUTCHER
RAND SORE LOAFER ME MISTER ICE-CREAM
DADDA DIM OOOOOOOOO I GOT SUCH A FRIGHT
I FLAKE TRY DOUBT — AFFERBECK LAUDER.
(20 marks)

(5) Translate the following into English:
You mask etcher hair cut, dear; Yuma sketcher rare cut,
dear; U. Masker chaw rare cart, dear; Yelljer steffter gair
chair cart, dear; Well lacquer dyno youra spaulder snegg?
You never take your Turbanoff — dear. (10 marks)

(6) Translate the following into Strine:
Did you know your left foot's missing?
Why, so it is. I wonder when that happened.
Isn't it painful?
Well, now that you mention it, I have been screaming a lot
lately.
Just show's you, doesn't it?
Well, since you put it that way, I suppose it does. (10
marks)

(7) What, if anything, do you find improbable about the
following?
He kissed her tenderly. 'Darling, your skin is like spung
gold, and your hair like a Pharaoh's pedal. Dearest, you are
Soap Rashes Toomey. I la few; arl nair fletchoo go.' With
grater motion he crushed a rinny zarms. Then he put on

his glasses, and looked at her more closely. He drew back in dismay. 'It's the wife. Crikey!' He kissed her once more, not quite so tenderly, saying, 'Look, fellas. No hands!' (5 marks)

(8) Write out in full the words of either of the following Strine songs:

(a) Ammonia vagabond lava, or (b) Ammonia burden a gilded cage. (10 marks)

(9) Who wrote the following? Translate into Strine:
'Dear Oedipus,' Jocasta said,
'Be jovial and jocose.
Let Mum take the worry
Out of being close.' (5 marks)

(10) Translate the following story into Strine, but first fill in the blanks, using any of the material appended:

It was midnight at Limehouse, and a quick brown fog jumped over the lazy docks. Snow White heard the sound of breaking glass echoing through the empty house. She heard the shot, and the muffled scream — then silence. She was trapped. 'Waddle-eye do?' she whispered, 'The secret sleek tout!' Slowly, the door opened, and .... appeared in the doorway. Even in the half light she could see the blood on his gloved hands, and ...., and the .... which he carried so nonchalantly. Suddenly .... appeared beside him, carrying .... 'Turner rand!' he barked. 'Wait!' He laughed cruelly. He took something from the pocket of his trenchcoat, and threw it at her feet. It was ....

Now select those of the following items which you think would be most appropriate, and fill in the blanks above:

81

An ear; a bag of manure from a well-rotted cow; a fac-
simile of 'The Blue Door', gift-wrapped, and bearing a
card with the words: 'Good luck, Reg. Get well soon. All
the best from your workmates at the sweatshop.'; a rattle-
waving baby boy dressed in pink; three half-inch Whit-
worth spanners; a diving helmet, complete with smiling
head; three witchety grubs in an elastic band; a cube of
very canned pineapple; the Loch Ness Monster as Hamlet;
two quandongs; a small bunch of tansy; something rather
nasty-looking which she couldn't identify in the half light,
but which looked sticky, and had beady little eyes; two
pairs of Grace Wade shoes; an Irish terrier with his mouth
full of carrageen; the man who broke the Bank of Monte
Carlo's auntie — I mean the one with twelve fingers who
suffered intermittently from herpes — the auntie, I mean,
not the fingers; a left foot, tattooed with the word 'Mother';
Little Dorrit with a hole in her forrit; three more diving
helmets; and the other foot. (20 marks)

(11) Complete the following Strine poem, and name the
author:
I musker danta the C.S.R., Ken,
So tie my ship tour buoy.
A norlye ask, is a gallon cask
Of overproof cocky's joy. (5 marks)

THE POSTMAN'S WHISTLE

I dreamed I heard the postman's whistle
Whistle like a scream.
I found, to my surprise, that his'll
Whistle like my dream.

The next day, at the Embassy,
I met Professor Lauder,
And heard him, to a member, say,
'Miss Gem, a poyna forda!'

That night I tried to dream in Strine,
And dream in Strine I did.
My dreams in Strine, I find, are fine;
I dreamed a mazzer kid.

    .   .   .   .   .

I dremm diurda postie swizzle
Wizzle liger scream.
Annizzle rogg-yer; E. sair zizzle
Wizzle like my dream.

THE CASE OF THE MISSING TORSO

'Skew smee, professor,' said Philippa Nibbly, scratching her ear with a pencil, 'but there's a gentleman atside waiting to see you.' A gentleman? I wondered who it could be; I don't know any gentlemen. I glanced at my diary to see if I was expecting any gentleman, but there was nothing before lunch except an almost illegible entry, apparently written by me without my knowledge, 'Sandra's birthday lemons check brake fluid.' A gentleman? Perhaps it was just another professor, and not a gentleman at all. Or perhaps it was someone from Hollywood, wanting to make a film about me. I wondered what they had in mind for the title; *The Hero of Dare Nunda*, perhaps, or *Lauder the Flies*. Or even *Birth of a Notion*. After all . . .

Miss Nibbly broke in on my dreams. 'I think he's a policeman,' she said, uneasily. 'He looks like a policeman.' Good lord, what had I done? I tried to recall if I had been in any hit-run incidents recently, or armed robberies. Had I concealed any torsos under the floorboards of the Department? I was relieved to find that my record, if not actually spotless, was — well, clean enough. As far as I could remember I hadn't even bashed anyone lately. I checked my pulse. It was almost back to normal. I came out from under the desk and sat in my chair again. 'Oh, police?' I said casually. 'Really? Ask him to come in.'

As he entered the room I could see at a glance that he was a policeman. A high-up one too; he had it written all over him. A big man, he looked competent and hard, and he had an unmistakable air of authority. Probably Assistant Commissioner. But why did he want to see *me*?

Whatever it was I would need to handle the situation very carefully, very tactfully. It would be best to treat the whole thing casually — with the lightheartedness of the innocent.

'Good morning, Assistant Commissioner. Ugh! Agh! Ooooooo — Ugh!' I had inadvertently shut my left little finger inside the desk drawer. I lit a pencil with a cigarette. 'And what can we do for you?' I asked him, 'No torsos under this floor, I'm afraid. Sorry to disappoint you. Ha ha ha.' I deftly extracted what was left of my little finger from the drawer. I stubbed out my pencil on the calendar, and offered him the diary: 'Smoke?' I wondered idly how I would feel if he did find a torso under the floor, or even a couple of legs, in a cupboard somewhere. There was a long and ominous silence. He stared at me open-mouthed and apparently alarmed.

'I muspy go anatomy mind,' he said. 'Yuper Fessor Lauder? Arno! I muspy inner wrong room, or I muspy gohen ranner bairnd.'

'No, no, Commissioner?' I promoted him — just to be on the safe side, 'You're in the right room. But there are no legs or anything like that here. No loot even. Nothing. Ha ha . . . ha. . . .'

'Look, perfessor,' he said. 'Muspy summer stike.' He handed me a card. Hoomit, Maik & Surne Pty Ltd, I read, Market Research, Mass Communications Review and Counsel, Statistical Analysis, Public Opinion and Relationship Bureau, Business and Management Consultants — Ogden Hoomit, Director. It was a big card; it had to be, but then he was a big man.

Really, I thought, I'll have to do something about Miss Nibbly — have to give her a good talking to. All this scare about police. Making a fool of me in front of strangers. Why, anyone could see at a glance that this was no policeman. Here was a serious student of mass communications and all that other stuff. A dedicated research worker like myself — a fellow scientist; he had it written all over him.

'My dear Mr Hoomit,' I said, 'I'm delighted to meet you at last. We've heard all about you of course, and the wonderful work you're doing down there at — I glanced at his card — at H.M. & S. Wonderful! Don't mind my little jokes about torsos; I mistook you for someone else. You look very much alike — almost identical, in fact, except that she's much smaller and walks with a limp. Breeds poodles, too — nice little woman. Do you know her?' I didn't know how to stop now. I offered him another cigarette. 'Miniatures,' I said. 'Poodles, I mean — not cigarettes; it's a king-size. Tell me more about this research now. Must be fascinating.'

He was staring at me again. He came to with a start as I pushed the cigarette into his open mouth and held a light in front of it. 'Kink's eyes? Poodles?' he said, not taking his eyes from me. 'What poodles?'

'Well, this girl I was telling you about. The one who looks so like you, I mean. You know — the one that limps? Well, these poodles of hers — the miniatures . . .' I stopped. This wasn't getting us anywhere. I couldn't afford to spend the whole morning talking about poodles to a complete stranger. Who did he think I was? It was ridiculous. I was a busy man, with a full programme ahead of me — Sandra's birthday and the lemons and everything.

'Look, let's start again,' I said. 'Tell me why you're here, and I'll tell you all about the poodles later — if we have time.'

He shrugged his shoulders, and shook his head in a dazed fashion. He took a drag at his cigarette. Gradually he seemed to collect his wits. He opened up an impressive-looking black leather case with an inbuilt filing system.

'Nowper fessor,' he started off, 'I wunner a fewpie good enough to answer a few questions. My commany spinker missioned by the mannerfecturers of (he named a well-known detergent) twassertain the exac percentage . . .'

I found my attention wandering swiftly. What the hell was all this about? '. . . Now we fine television viewers have, like yourself, bin moce quoprative. We finer fwee reely analyse the situation weaken put moce viewers innu one of at least fork adder grease. Now weraz the morgan serftif viewer may have certain predgersez, the morse fisterkited viewer, like your good self, will, on the other hand, be even mork worpative. Nowf we drawper graph — like so . . .' He had produced a pad of graph paper, and was now setting up a small adding machine on my desk. The situation was getting out of hand; we'd have been better off with the poodles. He talked incessantly while he worked at the graph. He made rapid calculations on the adding machine, and plotted in the figures of a spectacular curve.

'Core satsoni to give you a rah fidea of howt workzout, anna corsin ackshell practice, as I thing kule red leer gree, it soma cheesier . . .'

'Look, Mr Hoomit, I must tell you about these poodles.' I tried hard to regain control, but he just waved his left hand in my face in a tictac gesture, and raised his voice. 'Nowper fessor, jumine telling meek zackly what your considered opinion is of the last episode of *Necroman*.'

I had never seen *Necroman,* as we don't have TV, but he was so interested in his subject that I didn't have the heart to tell him.

'Brilliant,' I said. 'Brutal, mind you, and pornographic — but adultly so.' He looked pleased, and made lots of little marks on a chart in coloured inks.

'Ware lat zitcher see. Yair swee feel *Necroman* is reel adult entertainment. In fac my cummany spraird to be associated with *Necroman.* Nowper fessor, fewdone mine, arl leave this questionnaire with youffra feud eyes. Now hair batterfye call again say neck Smundy — No, Mundy's a puppy-collared eye. Say nex Chewsdy? Bat the same time? Or rat-shorken venience. Youjah say Wendell sou chew, anarl fit in. A corsile liaise with your seckertry. A now fewdone mine . . .' He started to open up further compartments in his case. How was I to get rid of him? He was indefatigable and apparently immovable. He was talking briskly about categories of viewers, and the social implications of *Necroman*. He explained also that his client's product washed out trapped grease by means of pulsier mini-bubbles, and that it was in every way a superior product, as was only to be expected from the sponsors of such adult entertainment as *Guess Whom*.

He continued to ask questions which I answered to the best of my ability, or rather in such a way as to cause a minimum of comment and delay. He filled in his charts and forms with lightning speed, and kept thanking me for being soak woprative.

'And now,' — he turned to me with a bright, sentimental smile — 'Hammany kiddies?'

I was about to supply him with the fictitious information he so obviously craved when Miss Nibbly appeared at the doorway. 'Skew smee, professor,' she said, scratching her ear with a pencil, 'but there's a gentleman atside, waiting to see you.' She looked a little uncomfortable. 'I think he's a policeman,' she added slowly.

'Good,' I said. 'Show him in right away. I'll be delighted to give him any information I can about this brutal murder. Mr Hoomit, I'm afraid I'll have to ask you to leave. This is a matter of life and death. The Assistant Commissioner needs my help. You'll appreciate that I cannot possibly keep him waiting. I'm sorry but you'll have to leave immediately. Yes, yes, I know; the questionnaire. Just give it to Miss Nibbly on your way out.' I picked up his adding machine and crammed it into his case. The various loose papers, graphs and charts which he had strewn all over my desk I forced into his hands, into his pockets — anywhere. In a matter of a few seconds I had him completely packed up, out of the door and on his way. I sank back in the chair and sighed with relief. Thank heavens, peace at last.

Now, I suppose I'd better see this new visitor. I laughed to myself. I wondered who this 'policeman' would turn out to be. Life assurance, perhaps, or encyclopaedias.

A tall, heavily built man entered the room, followed by two more of equal omnipotence and menace. 'Professor Lauder,' he said, 'I want to ask you a few questions in connection with the discovery, in this building early this morning, of a dismembered female torso . . .'

SUCH A GOOD BOY

He never said 'Die' to the living.
He never said 'Scat' to a cat.
He never said 'Boo' to a kangaroo.
He never did this — or that.

He always kept clear of propellors;
Never spoke to the man at the wheel.
He always said 'Thanks' to people in banks,
And always took food with his meal.

He never took umbrage, or opium,
Or ran round the rugged rocks.
He never missed school, or acted the fool,
And always wore woollen socks.

He never sat on a tuffet,
Or pulled out a plum with his thumb;
And never, in churches, left ladies in lurches;
Or opened the OP *rum.*

He never pinched little girls' bottoms,
Or peered down the front of their necks;
Considered it folly to covet a dolly,
Or think of the opposite sex.

He never did anything nasty.
He never got stinking, or cried;
Unmarred by one speckle, a permanent Jekyll
With never a shadow of Hyde.

He never called anyone 'Drongo',
Or even ate peas with a knife.
He never crossed swords with the overlords;
Such a good boy all his life.

When he finally died and was buried
His loving ones tried to mourn;
They put at his head a tablet which read,
'Here he lies, but why was he born?'

THE STRINE SONG

Tim Pannelli, the famous poet and songwriter, telephoned me recently and asked if he might call and see me; he wanted my advice about a Strine song he had written. Naturally, I told him I'd be delighted, and so, here he was now in my office. I had, of course, read most of Pannelli's work, including the many historical dramas for which he is famous, but until now I had never had the pleasure of meeting this great man.

Tim Pannelli is a most unusual-looking man. Powerfully built, and I would think at least seven feet tall in his stockinged feet, he is not handsome in the usual sense of the word, but he is certainly impressive.

As I rose to greet him I noticed that his open, friendly face was marred by an ugly welt of scar tissue across the forehead, caused, I later discovered, by his continual failure to stoop when passing through doorways. Apart from that, his head appeared to be one of the standard, unshrunken ones, with the finely chiselled nose and all that. One could see immediately that here was a great artist, a dedicated poet. He was smoking an extraordinarily malodorous cigar, and he had, apparently, recently consumed a fairly large amount of garlic.

'My dear Mr Pannelli,' I said. 'This is a great pleasure.'

He smiled in response to my greeting, and I noticed the elegant crenellations of his mossy nicoteeth.

'No, no, Professor Lauder,' he replied, 'the pleasure is mine. It's very good of thou to see me. I know thou must be a very busy man.'

I was momentarily puzzled by his use of the second person singular, and then I remembered all those historical dramas.

'I am most anxious,' he continued, 'to have thy expert criticism. This is my first song in Strine, and, as thou know, it's not an easy language.'

'Of course,' I said. 'But do sit down. Will you have a cup of coffee or a three-course meal or something?' I was hoping to be able to detach him from that cigar, which was about ten inches long and as black as licorice.

'No thank thee — just had lunch.' He exhaled enthusiastically. I opened the windows. He continued, 'Well, I mustn't take up too much of thy time. To work, to work.' He patted his pockets, searching for his song. There was something magnetic about the man's personality; one couldn't help liking him, in spite of the cigar.

'Ah, here it is,' he cried. 'Oh, and have some of this. Very good for thee.' He offered me a handful of garlic.

'No thanks, just had lunch,' I said.

'Well, if thou are ready, I'll sing it now. Thou haven't a piano, have thou? No? Never mind.'

'Just a moment,' I said. 'Do you mind if I call my assistant? I know he would want to hear this. And Miss Nibbly, too. They'd never forgive me if I didn't share this unique experience with them.' I called Miss Nibbly and asked her to tell Dr Paragon to come in. I introduced everyone, and then we all sat down on the floor at Pannelli's stockinged feet.

He drew himself up to his full height, and held out his bit of paper at arm's length. He paused for a moment, then took a deep breath.

'One, two, three, testing,' he sang in a surprisingly light, clear tenor voice. 'One, two, three, testing. How's that, okay?'

'Magnificent,' I said. Dr Paragon nodded his head.

'Skew smee,' said Miss Nibbly, 'you've got a rarely laughly voice, Mr Pannelli, but I rarely think it'd sand even better if you took out your cigar. Don't you think so, Dr Paragon?'

Andy looked up from the hot dog he was eating. 'Yair, stairfnittly,' he said. 'Yair sarn daddedly. Snow datter battered.'

Pannelli removed his cigar from his mouth and put it down carefully on the edge of the desk, where it continued to crackle briskly. 'Okay,' he said, 'let's go. With Air Chew. That's the title of the song — With Air Chew. Ah one, ah two, ah three, ah four.' And he started to sing.

> *'With air chew, with air chew,*
> *Iker nardly liver there chew,*
> *An I dream a badger kisser snite and die.*
> *Phoney wicked beer loan,*
> *Jars-chewer mere nonnair roan,*
> *An weed dreamer batter mooner pinner sky.*
>
> *'With air chew, with air chew,*
> *Hair mike-owner liver there chew?*
> *Wile yerrony immy dream sigh maulwye scrine.*
> *Anna strewer seffner barf,*
> *Yuma snow-eye Nietzsche laugh,*
> *Cars with air chew immy arm sit snow-ewe Strine.'*

When he had finished there was a long silence. I think we were all too overcome by our feelings to applaud. Miss Nibbly had broken down completely, and was sobbing and blowing her nose. Even Dr Paragon, who ordinarily doesn't show any emotion other than impatience, was visibly affected. He sniffed hard, and surreptitiously brushed away a tear with the back of his hot-dog. It was a moving and memorable experience. In the general commotion, while we were all scrambling to our feet, and coughing and carrying on, I removed the great man's cigar from my desk and dropped it into a filing cabinet.

We all crowded around him and patted him on the back and congratulated him. Miss Nibbly asked for his autograph, and Dr Paragon offered him a chlorophyll tablet.

'Ye think it's okay, then?' asked Pannelli.

'Truly magnificent,' I said. 'I wouldn't think of altering a word of it. And I must compliment on your Strine accent. Remarkable.' Miss Nibbly blew her nose again, and went to get some coffee.

'Thou don't think the title is perhaps a little too — ah, abrupt? I had thought of calling it *Phoney Eiche Daffer Latin Slamp.*'

'No, I wouldn't touch it,' I said. 'With Air Chew is just right; so much more direct; so poignant.' I kept on talking, to keep his mind from his cigar, but already he was patting his pockets again. Fortunately Miss Nibbly came in before he could light up, and we all sat down and drank the coffee, and talked about With Air Chew.

'Welimer sconow,' said Dr Paragon, finally breaking it up. 'Car morn Philippa, back twirk. Well taddar sport. Be senior.'

The spell was broken. Pannelli looked at his watch.

'Well,' he said, 'Thank thee again for all thy advice and encouragement. Thou've been most helpful.' He shook me warmly by both hands, and left. There was a dull thud of bone on architrave as he reached the doorway outside.

WITH AIR CHEW

NOSE TONE UNTURNED

And the Secretary is desirous (the letter went on to say, as well as I remember) that I should inform you of the Minister's appreciation of the valuable contribution you are making to a wider understanding of our glorious heritage — the Strine language. He refers, in particular, to a public statement you have recently made to the effect that all literature addressed to intending migrants to Australia should be published in two languages, English and Strine. And so on. It was signed by Victor Cluster, First Assistant Secretary of the Department of Inducement and Assimilation.

I had pointed out, in my statement to the press, that the initial dismay and subsequent disillusion of some newly arrived migrants to this country could be obviated by making it clear to them, before they leave their native land, that although English is the official, written language of this country, the unofficial, spoken language is Strine.

Anyway, the Minister had, it seems, decided to take the matter up and, to use his own unique and tersely cogent phrase, to 'leave no stone unturned'. I was invited to Canberra to discuss the matter and, after due deliberation, to make detailed recommendations to the Minister.

I managed to have a few words with Dr Cluster before the others arrived. He told me that the only other persons who would be attending this initial discussion would be the chairman, Professor Mingle, representing the Minister; Professor Blare of Airdelight University; and, of course, himself. He warned me quietly that Professor Blare was not a particularly easy man to get along with. 'In fact he's an intractable bloody nong,' he said tactfully. 'But the Minister feels that he might well be able to make a valuable contribution because of his particularly pure Strine accent.'

He had barely finished speaking, and the word 'nong' was still echoing among the teacups, when the door was flung open, and Professor Blare, followed by an already rather desperate-looking chairman, burst into the room. He threw his hat onto the desk, knocking over a large, silver-framed portrait of Mrs Cluster with a spaniel. He shook Dr Cluster's hand so boisterously that I could hear the bones crunching like biscuits. He ignored me completely. He stumbled over a chair, tore at his collar, and shouted, 'Now Warsaw liss Strine chairs? I carmike hatter tiler fit. A noo sis Zafflepock repbairg, or worreffris snime is? Dar sneeno hatter spairl?' We were off to a very inauspicious start.

There was a lot of embarrassed shuffling and coughing, and Dr Cluster tried to disappear into the floor. I could see now what he had meant; but Professor Blare, for all his madcap gaucherie, might well turn out to be very valuable indeed; his accent was bang-on.

While I was saying hullo to Professor Mingle, I saw Dr Cluster saying a few quiet words into Professor Blare's whiskery ear. He immediately turned to me with an enormous, glary, foxy grin, and crushed my hand in his instant meatpress.

'Sorry, mate,' he screamed with laughter, sucking in great bagfuls of air through his clacky tombstone teeth, and showering out spluttery droplets all over my face. 'Dint Noah's you mate. Glatter meecher. An woss your rill nime? Carmorn carmorn dopey shy.' He jabbed at my sternum with a case-hardened forefinger, and leered at me with pale blue popping eyes.

'Well, actually . . .' I started to tell him, but he was off again, fizzing about the room, waving his arms, knocking things over, and telling some long, unfunny story about his wartime sex life. 'An theshy wars praggly nygerd . . .' he was saying. Eventually he was brought under control by the chairman, and we got down to work.

After the preliminary formalities, I was asked if I would elaborate on the statement I had already made. We each had a copy of this in front of us, but of course Blare hadn't read his, and we had to wait while he wrestled with it noisily; squirming, clearing his throat, and scratching at his crusty, sunburned scalp. He looked up every now and then, as if he found our silence unbearable, and bared his tigerish fangs, and said, 'Haaaaa, Haaaaaaam, Ha!' Then he would suck in some more air, and get down again to his task. I don't think he got past the first paragraph — in fact I wonder, now, if he can read. But he put on a good show. After a few minutes he placed the paper slowly and deliberately on the table in front of him; he lifted his hands high into the air, very quickly, as though he had just completed building a house of cards. He slapped his thighs triumphantly, and said, 'Haaaaaaa!' and with the back of his hand he wiped his chin with the wild flourish of someone escaping from slavery, and again he said, 'Haaaaaaa!' He must have used up more energy in five minutes than anyone else would in a week. The chairman caught my eye.

'Well, gentlemen,' I said, 'I have nothing to add to the statement in front of you. I believe, however, that with Professor Blare's help I can make out a fairly strong case for bilingual literature for migrants. I propose to take at random a few typical situations, such as a newcomer might be expected to encounter, and — well, just let's see what happens.'

Professor Blare, I noticed, had temporarily abandoned the realistic drawing he had been working on of a naked woman, and was now chewing busily at a loose thread at his shirt cuff button. He bit it off and spat it out noisily.

He looked up as I paused; he obviously hadn't listened to a word I had been saying.

'Wossat, mate?' He held up his drawing for everyone to admire, and screamed with laughter. 'Noppaird, eh?'

'Well,' I continued, 'first of all, let us imagine, say, a young English girl (Blare looked up quickly, eyebrows raised), new to this country, and recently married to an Australian. It is the middle of the night. Suddenly she sits up in bed in their new home somewhere in the outer suburbs. She is nervous; she thinks she has heard someone at the door. Okay? Got that, professor?'

'Look, snore ma juice cowny gone me, mate. You know youger tadder the wire these sorter things.' He scratched his leg cruelly, and went back to his drawing — flower pots now, and little squares with dots in them.

The chairman looked tired. Cluster was drumming his fingertips softly on the table.

'Well,' I battled on, wondering if we'd be given a drink before lunch, 'well, if she were still at home at Surbiton, or Welwyn Garden City, what would she say to her husband in this situation? She'd say: George, there's someone there. Now who can that be, knocking on the door at this time of night? It's half past two! But if she says this to her Australian husband he just looks at her blankly and goes back to sleep. Naturally, the poor girl is then overwhelmed by despondency and alarm, and starts to make plans to go home to Mum and the smog. What has happened is that her husband doesn't know what she's saying because she has been talking English instead of Strine.' I paused, to let this sink in. Professor Blare's stomach rumbled violently. 'Pahn *mee!*' he said.

'Now, professor, if I may have your attention for a moment, what should she have said?'

He looked at me as though I had just arrived from Mars. 'Wossat, mate?'

Then, suddenly, I thought I could see how it might be

done. 'Professor,' I said, 'would you please just repeat what I say?'

'Okay, sport. Any time.'

'George,' I said, 'there's someone at the door outside.'

'Where, mate?' He looked over his shoulder.

'No, no, professor. Just repeat what I say. Right? George, there's someone at the door outside.'

'George.' He stopped. No one moved. Somewhere, in the passage outside, a pin dropped. He looked at us each in turn. Slowly, he smiled.

'George,' he said, 'the summer gnat the door rat's-eyed.'

'Oh, wonderful!' I said. 'Good!' Everyone relaxed. The chairman lit a cigarette.

'Now, are you ready? Now who can that be, knocking on the door at this time of night?'

'Nahoogen thappy?' said the professor, 'nogger nonner dort this timer night? Haaaaa. Hmmmmm. Haaaaaaam!' At last he appeared to have caught on; he had even stopped squirming.

'It's half past two,' I said.

'Note za-pa sleffen mate,' he said, looking at his watch.

'No, no, professor. Just repeat what I say. Go and see who it is, George, it must be important.'

'Norm,' said the professor, 'it zapa stoo. Goan see hootiz, Norm. Muspeem pawnt.' He paused, and added anxiously, 'Mipey re lurgent!'

He was inspired. How could he possibly have known that the Strine for George is Norm? Pure intuition, obviously. I took a quick look at the others. Dr Cluster's joyful mouth was wide open. Professor Mingle was leaning back with his eyes closed, his hands folded across his stomach. He looked as though he were listening to Mozart.

'Ready, professor? Now — We've got a new car, Betty. You wouldn't believe it would you?'

'Weegar newgar, Cherryl. You woomba leaver twoocha? Carmen air flooker tit.' He was really in the groove now.

102

'A mitre mine scotter new Vailiant.' His eyes had taken on a fixed and glassy look.

'What did he do with the old car?' I asked.

'Thair tole hape? Eager tridderfit.' His eyes were rolling back into his head and he appeared to be going into some sort of trance. I thought I would try him on some more advanced stuff. 'Where,' I said, 'is the pen of my aunt?'

'Wezzme Auntie Spiro?'

'There's no drink left, Doris.'

'We fra natter grog, Sandra.' He was now in a deep trance. I whispered to the chairman, and Dr Cluster tiptoed out and came back with a tape recorder. Now we were really in business.

'There's no more pudding, dear,' I said, in a high, feminine falsetto.

'Welker knife some bren jairm then, marm?' He jiggled an invisible yo-yo with a rigid right arm. 'An marm marm. War wego navver tea, marm?' And so it went on.

By about six o'clock we had all had enough. The three of us were sprawled at the table, finishing off the last of a bottle of scotch. The professor was lying on the floor in a coma.

Jack (Professor Mingle) sat up and yawned slowly. He stretched himself and rolled down his sleeves. Vic Cluster held the bottle up to the light, then he put on his shoes.

'Well, gentlemen,' said the chairman, putting on his coat, and tugging at his tie. 'A very fruitful day. The Minister will be delighted.' He looked anxiously at Professor Blare, who had now begun to snore gently and was, I was relieved to see, scratching himself in his sleep. His lips were twitching, like a dreaming dog's.

We all looked at each other. Vic hid the glasses and the empty bottle, and tidied up the room. Then he went over and shook the professor gently.

'Wake up, professor,' he said quietly. 'Time to catch your plane soon.'

The professor stirred, and opened his pale blue eyes. He sat up slowly.

'Woskoa non?' he asked.

'You had a bit of a blackout, professor,' I told him. 'Nothing serious, but we thought you ought to rest for a while. How do you feel now?'

'Noppaird, mate. Not reel bad.' He looked at us all suspiciously, then at his watch. 'Neely ah-pa *seeegs*!' he screeched. 'I carber leevit.' He got slowly to his feet. He looked a bit staggery. I would never have believed he could be so subdued.

We got him a cup of coffee, and he finished off the remains of some sandwiches. Gradually he came back to life. We all went off to the airport together and, by the time his plane had arrived, he was right back in top form; talking our heads off, booming and spluttering, and sucking at his great sharky fangs.

STRINE RHYMES FOR KIDDIES

Rider cock horse to Nyngan or Nome,
To seer fine lady clee natter Rome;
Mo Nyngan grow Nyngan fee tawler blister,
Sheesha lav music upon a transistor.

Little Chair Corner come blow your horn,
An dofer get those sharps and flats;
Ando calm beckon Christma Smorn
In wunner those silly paper hats.

The war slittle chap, panny adder little nap,
An his dinner was long overdone.
His good wife Nelly was stillet the telly,
With Astroboy, Steptoe, and Son.

Hi diddle diddle, Little Jenny Baker.
Heigh ho! says Rowley, waddle-eye do with me pence?
Me mumma wozza Quaker; tiger ruppen shaker;
Now say it all again slowly;
It doesn't seem to scan or even make sense.

ORDEAL BY EARBASH

'Well yugen dooitcher like,' said Dr Paragon, in his usual uncompromising manner. 'Zarf trawlitz your show. Bargee, mite, I moany triner mica teasier.'

'Yes, I know, Andy,' I said, 'and I appreciate your thoughtfulness on my behalf, but . . .'

'Listen, mite,' he cut in, 'I jar swan a get it over. Iger tarder Stan a *nar* Paula time. Orlis farsova a lotta my-grinse. Y. carnay learner talk Strine before they *car* mere?'

'Okay,' I said. 'Put it down with the others.'

He lowered the large notice he had been holding up over his head, and banged it down onto the floor. He stood there, muttering, and waving the blood back into his hands. 'Thing kyle goa navver bye tweet,' he said. *'Ear* fats okay with *ewer* course,' he added with heavy sarcasm.

'Yes, Andy, you go and have some lunch.'

'Seer lighter then.' He went off, muttering something about aorta do this and Y. carnay do that.

I turned the notice around and propped it up against the wall so that it faced into the room. I stood well back and looked at it critically. Yes, it looked about right to me. It was one of a series of bilingual notices which I was preparing, at the request of the Department of Inducement and Assimilation, for display in Australia House, in London. Now that the authorities had decided, at last, that all official signs and notices in this country were to be in two languages, English and Strine, it was important that intending migrants to Australia should be given, in advance, some idea of the sort of thing they could expect to be confronted by on arrival.

The notice in front of me was three feet wide by two feet deep, with black lettering on a brilliant yellow ground. The English wording appeared immediately above the Strine translation:

NO ADMITTANCE

Key Powder Vere — Penalty £5 $10

The $10 had purposely been lettered in a different style from the remainder of the wording, and had been placed out of alignment, so as to give the whole thing an official, asymmetric, authoritative appearance.

I looked at my watch. I'd have to skip lunch; Kangruskin would be here soon. I asked Miss Nibbly to get me a baked bean and potato salad sandwich, on white bread, and a carton of lemon flavoured milk — the usual professorial snack. Then I stood all the notices up, side by side against the walls, and sat back and admired them while I waited for my sandwich.

Eli Kangruskin's background was something of a mystery. He had told me that his father was a Russian, and his mother Hungarian; that he had been born in Paris, and had spent most of his childhood travelling with his parents all over Europe, and in this way had learned to speak ten languages. I had heard elsewhere that he was born in Liverpool, and that his parents were Greek. Whatever the facts were, he certainly spoke at least ten European languages — but each with the accent of the country he had just previously left. He spoke Italian like a native — a native, that is, of Copenhagen. He spoke practically no Strine at all, presumably because he was still here in Australia. He had arrived in this country a few years ago, having come from Birmingham or somewhere, where he had been engaged, so he said, in some top secret liaison work for the British Government. In Australia he had worked at a number of different jobs: growing mushrooms in a disused tunnel, driving a bulldozer, sandpapering the lips of window display models, stringing beads, and running what he called a 'fish coffee'. Finally he had joined the Department as a specialist in languages; and now, today, he was here to go through this latest batch of notices. I had found him, during our brief association, to be co-operative and friendly, and we got on quite well together. However he seemed to get on Dr Paragon's nerves — but then, who didn't? His main trouble was that once he started talking he was unable to stop, and what he had to say was not always relevant.

'He are, sport,' Andy was saying, 'Smoke? He are, air fwunner mine.'

'North airnx,' said Kangruskin. 'Ah dawn's mork. Munjew, woonts ah woss a gent's morka. Boot ah harder giffit oop; ah woss korphenorla tarm. Ahra mamba, one Sorbonne a tarm, whan ah woss a student in Paris, ah shed a flutt with a chupp colled Funton. Chorlie Funton. Eeeeee, he wosser narse chupp. Well, woun dair — it wosser Moondair; ahra mamba it wosser Moondair because it was rairnen. . . .' He was off to his usual flying start.

'Here's the next one, Frad,' I said. He had asked me to call him Frad, although his name was supposed to be Eli. He said all his France called him Frad. I drew his attention, such as it was, to the notice:

BEWARE OF ONCOMING TRAFFIC
War Chaffer Ong-calming Veagles

'Ooooo! Fair skluss,' said Kangruskin. 'Fair skluss. Remarned smee offer tarm wenwee webber harnd the larns utter plairce colled Doonkairk — you mayor foorder fit. Anywhere, we werrin dairnger of bing cuptured. Muppler toon hud joospin . . .'

'Yes, yes, okay sport,' broke in Andy, impatient as

ever but trying, not very successfully, to conceal it. 'Fit sorla sime to you — hair bat jar sketter non wither business in hairnd?' He held the next notice up in front of Kangruskin's nose:

PLEASE DO NOT SMOKE

Nouse mogen!

'Norse Morgan,' said Kangruskin. 'Eeeeee! Fair skluss. Air worn! Core Sardon's mork mussalf. Booter ramamba, a frantomarn . . . It woss whan ah wossin Frimmundle. This chupp wosser grairt frand — an awl frantomarn. Anywhere, he yoost to smawg a parp. Well woundair, he was teginny swarf . . . Munjew, he harden bin murried morna coopler moonce. His warf snairm, fie ramamba corrairctly, woss Gluddis. Well, anywhere . . .'

'Next one, Andy, please,' I said. One thing about Kangruskin — he didn't mind in the least being interrupted, or even ignored. Just as long as he had a face near him — even a good photograph would do — he'd go on talking.

PLEASE DO NOT SPIT

Do Not Spit!

'Saw anywhere . . . arsy stairpt insard, soodenleh orla lart scare-morn. Unna corsy got soocha frarty brawkie sparp. Snupp kleenorfinny stairth. Kloock! Anywhere, the neg stair — it wosser Soondair. Und soy sair twis warf, he sairt, Gluddis, he sairt, he sairt, Gluddis, arf brawken me parp, a nitzer Soondair. . . .'

'Or geemite, car morn, car morn, zarp tew. Gaudy drivey arp the wall.' Andy appeared to be losing control. 'Hi, you! Jar sloogered the notice willier? Look! Jar slemmy poodger inner pidger. Gawd, I mire swell noppy hear. Torga bat disinterested. . . .'

VISITORS ARE REQUESTED NOT TO WALK ON THE LAWNS
Key Porpha Gra Smite — An Don't Pigger Flares

Kangruskin nodded in a vague way at the wording. I don't think he was aware now of anything but the magic of his own monologue. Andy had to, or thought he had to prod him in the chest. 'See? Key porpha gra smite!' he shouted in his face. 'Lougar fattabatta narf a this; woddsy thinky *zear* for?'

'Ooooo! Eeeeee! Fair skluss! Anywhere, Gluddis — yus, thutt wosser nairm, Gluddis. Ahra mamba naw, Gluddis. Anywhere, arsett wosser Soondair, orla poobs wek lawsed. Well, anywhere — Ooooo, it mooster bin a coopler moon slairter, wenner woss buck in Frimmundle. Nought mooster bin foor moon slairter; ahra mamba because it wosser Wairnstair un ah woss barn a noo oomprulla. Eeeee, nought lark the awld worn thaw. Or naw, nought lark the awld worn. The awld worn wosser leetle fawlder narp worn. It tairter leetle norp on the hundle. Here, I shaw you. Dew huffer bit a pairper? Uh leetle silfer norp. . . .'

DANGER! SUPRNTNDNT TRNSPT RESRCH STN
Loogairdy Dome Bycher!

This one had been Andy's contribution, and consequently he had a proprietary attitude towards it. 'Look, sport,' he said slowly, enunciating each syllable with great care, 'Jar stoomie a fiver willier? Jar sloogered the bloody notice, and let sav your ont's depinion. Neff my norlis Gluddis-bull.' He had loosened his collar and tie, and was breathing hard and muttering, 'Gordger woomba leaver twoocha? Anew tell me I undress to mate his intelligence. Hi! You! *Look!*' He shouted, and jumped up and down. Then he put his fingers into his mouth and let out an ear-splitting whistle. I sometimes wonder about Andy; probably something to do with his toilet-training. Or perhaps it's his glands. Anyway, whatever the initial cause may have been, his top, today, was rapidly approaching blowpoint.

DANGER! KEEP CLEAR OF THE PROPELLORS

Hey, Ewes! Yorpha Bittner Go Nither Skruse

'But wed a Mormon tum's tairl you. Heewee were bug in Fairness. You naw, Fairness? All Fairness — E. Neatly? Anywhere, arse aired to this chupp — this corned lair chupp. Arse air twim, uss-et, we warner gorta the Dodger's Pulse, ussairt. But or liquored sair woss, Cissy Norrie, Cissy Norrie. Itcher's captain sairn cissy norrie cissy norrie cissy norrie. Um paw awl Chorlie Funton — corsy woss blarn droonk, munjew — blarn droonk. He kep sairny waunted fallen tears. Ah worn fallen tears, he sairt. Men, he sairt. He sairt, Men, ah Moor-stuffer bort fife fallen tears. Naw ah usk you! Saw you naw wodder sair twim? Heh, heh, heh. Ah sair twim. Heh heh heh . . . Naw you womb Belair fit. Buttered straw . . . a new mare quart me. Arset, cissy norrie cissy norrie cissy norrie. Heeeeeeeee, heeeeeeeee, heeeeeeeee. . . . Dog abort luff. . . .'

IT IS REGRETTED THAT, OWING TO
CIRCUMSTANCES BEYOND THE JURISDICTION
OF THIS DEPARTMENT, FURTHER
INFORMATION HAS BECOME TEMPORARILY
NON-AVAILABLE TO APPLICANTS

Gnome or Gnus! Calm Bear Klyter!